Éilís Ní Dhuibhne was born in Dublin. She was educated at University College Dublin and has a BA in English and a PhD in Irish Folklore. She worked for many years as a librarian and archivist in the National Library of Ireland and has taught on the MA for Creative Writing at University College Dublin and for the Faber Writing Academy. The author of more than twenty books, including six collections of short stories, several novels, children's books, plays and many scholarly articles and literary reviews, her work includes *The Dancers Dancing*, *The Shelter of Neighbours* and *Fox, Swallow, Scarecrow*. She has been the recipient of many literary awards, among them the Stewart Parker award for Drama, three Bisto awards for her children's books, several Oireachtas awards for novels in Irish, the PEN Award for Outstanding contribution to Irish Literature, and a Hennessy Hall of Fame Award. Her novel, *The Dancers Dancing* (Blackstaff, 1999; new edition 2007), was shortlisted for the Orange Prize for Fiction. One of Ireland's most important short story writers, Ní Dhuibhne's stories have appeared in many anthologies and have been widely translated. She is a member of Aosdána and President of the Folklore of Ireland Society.

D1077545

Éilís Ní Dhuibhne

Twelve Thousand Days

A Memoir of
Love and Loss

First published in 2018 by Blackstaff Press
an imprint of Colourpoint Creative Ltd
Colourpoint House
Jubilee Business Park
21 Jubilee Road
Newtownards BT23 4YH

With the assistance of the Arts Council of Northern Ireland

LOTTERY FUNDED

pg ix: Philip Larkin, 'Days', from *The Whitsun Weddings* (Faber, 1964),
reproduced by kind permission of Faber and Faber Limited.

pg 80: Philip Larkin, from 'Annus Mirabilis', from *High Windows*
(Faber, 1974), reproduced by kind permission of Faber and Faber Limited.

pg 189: Penelope Lively, from *Ammonites & Leaping Fish: A Life in Time*
(Penguin, 2013), reproduced by kind permission of David Higham Associates.

Printed and bound by CPI Group UK Ltd, Croydon CRO 4YY

A CIP catalogue for this book is available from the British Library

ISBN 978 1 78073 173 5

www.blackstaffpress.com

For my grandchildren,
Freja, Sadhbh and Niko

CONTENTS

PART ONE

PART TWO

Days

What are days for?
Days are where we live.
They come, they wake us
Time and time over.
They are to be happy in:
Where can we live but days?

Ah, solving that question
Brings the priest and the doctor
In their long coats
Running over the fields.

Philip Larkin

PART ONE

DAY 1

Arctic explorers

'You are an Arctic explorer!'

Twelve thousand days ago.

Bo had a wide range of colourful expressions in the form of proverbs and quotations. They spanned several languages. Most of the expressions were traditional, but they were augmented by adages and metaphors of his own invention. He had his favourites: 'Much squealing and little wool, as the woman said when they killed the pig.' 'Every little helps, as the wren said when she pissed in the sea.' Or, 'We have nothing to fear but fear itself.' Like a person's language or accent, these sayings were part of his personality; they constituted an element of his voice. No matter how often I heard these phrases, they retained their shine, and added life and colour to bland sentences. And they stuck in the memory when much else was forgotten.

Perhaps you could describe a person who cared enough about conversation to enliven it with sparkling formulae as an oral poet? Everyone needs formulae, and most people possess them, wittingly or not, but Bo had selected his arsenal of handy phrases with care – possibly because he was speaking one foreign language or another for most of his life, rather than his native Swedish. He told me once that when you are beginning to speak a new language it's useful to learn some colourful idioms that can be used in lots of different contexts. For instance, *'Just så ligger det till'* in Swedish, as an alternative to 'I agree' or – the usual resort of the learner – '*Ja*'. It means you don't have to think and translate laboriously all the time in the early crucial stages of learning; it gives you confidence, and may impress native speakers.

I wasn't an Arctic explorer, and had no intention of ever being one. I was scared of dogs, and, according to Bo, huskies can be especially vicious, even if you escape the attention of the polar bears. But I was a person who believed, when I was young, that I would much rather travel than stay at home and had been an armchair explorer from childhood. 'Explorer' is a nice word, an uplifting word, a word anyone would like to have used in a description of themselves. The kind of word that might crop up, if you were lucky, in your obituary.

The day he said that, Bo was in his office in college, at a little grey Formica-topped table in the corner by the door. There was an important mahogany table sitting like a dark lake in the middle of the room, with glass bookcases of impressive-looking volumes behind it, but he had set up this satellite for himself, and mostly worked at the ordinary kitchen table in the corner, crouching over it.

Not that Bo looked ordinary at all. Or humble. This was the thing about him. Although he could be reserved and considered himself shy, he projected energy and confidence. He was tall and broad-shouldered, with long arms, long legs and long musician's fingers. Profoundly blue eyes and a big aquiline nose – Roman, or maybe Norman is a more flattering and more accurate description. Full lips and a wide, frequent smile. His teeth were uneven and streaked with brown stains because he had smoked incessantly for twenty-odd years but that didn't stop him smiling. Coffee-coloured hair fell in a thick, untidy fringe over his forehead – he was forever pushing it back, or even, absent-mindedly, combing it back with a little plastic tortoiseshell comb that shared his breast pocket with a selection of pens and pencils. Always a pencil since he would die rather than mark a book with ink but you must always be ready and prepared to mark something interesting or useful in the book you're reading. He wore glasses, the big black-framed glasses of the seventies, and, usually, a Donegal tweed jacket – what in those days was called a sports coat.

But today he had taken off the jacket.

It was warm.

It was the start of summer.

It was May.

'Yes,' I said.

I was going not to the Arctic but to Denmark. A place nobody went to. A place everyone thought was boring – although opinion swerved into a U-turn as soon as Copenhagen was mentioned. Denmark sounded flat, square and dull. Bacon and butter and the Common Market. Copenhagen bubbled with fairy-tale promise, Hollywood romance. Elegant steeples, green and yellow houseboats on toytown canals. The song has a lot to do with it. And 'The Little Mermaid'. Danny Kaye and Hans Christian Andersen. And the sweet lyrical tune of the name itself, in its English version: Cop-en-hag-en. Meaning merchants' port, which gets you back to the Common Market and bacon and butter.

I had applied for a scholarship to this plain-sounding country with the magical capital. Decades before study years abroad became commonplace, Bo recommended his graduate students broaden their horizons, that they become explorers and wanderers, as he had been himself. He stuck up posters about scholarships on the noticeboard in the hall of his department in college and told students they should avail of the opportunities. Fill in the forms! Apply! Half his life was spent writing references. And the students responded; almost all of them went somewhere. The majority applied to Norway or Finland. They were the interesting-sounding places. The names had a ring to them. Grieg and Sibelius. They knew about Antti Aarne, the great Finnish folklorist, and maybe Asbjørnsen and Moe, who collected Norwegian stories. They had seen a play by Ibsen in the Focus Theatre. Fjords and lakes, ice and snow. Yes, naturally everyone wanted to go to Finland or Norway.

Sweden was third choice.

Nobody even bothered to apply to Denmark.

That wasn't why I picked it, although it would have been a sensible reason. Just like everyone else, I would have selected Norway, because of the fjords, and following that, Finland – the name sounds like the tinkle of silver bells, like mountain water dancing down a green hillside. *Oh, Finlandia!* I chose Denmark because it was the only place left when I decided to apply, just after my boyfriend, Oliver, broke off our engagement, and told me I was an opinionated feminist and that he was in love with somebody else – half the women in Belfield, it seemed. By the time he got around to telling me all this, the deadlines for Finland and Norway and Sweden had passed.

Today the letter had come informing me that my application had been successful. So I was going to give up my job in the National Library and go to Denmark for a year.

Bo wondered if I could get leave of absence from the library.

'I don't think so.'

It didn't seem important. When you are twenty-four, a year has no end. You know it can extend to infinity.

I had been working in the library for almost a year. That had felt like a century. It was quite long enough. To Bo, as to most people, being an Assistant Keeper in the National Library of Ireland sounded like a good job for a scholarly and bookish person. Everyone just adored the library: the charming portico supported by fat columns of Portland stone, sheltering from the rain with the readers and librarians who gathered on the steps to smoke and chat. The splendid reading room with its baize-trimmed oak desks and pretty green lamps! And surely to spend your day among all those lovely old books must be so inspiring and uplifting.

Not really.

I had no intention of going back once I made my escape.

My ambition was to finish my PhD and get an academic job, teaching and doing research. An *interesting* job. I had been offered an interesting job in the university in Oran two years ago, when I finished my MPhil, but I had turned it down, on account of Oliver. 'Don't go,' he said. Instead, I took a job in the Civil Service, which was the last thing I wanted. Now I regretted the decision. Obviously: the relationship with Oliver was over, and the opportunity to go to Algeria was long gone.

Like all doctoral students, I loved my subject, I loved research and analysis. As much as I needed air and food, I longed for a job that was engaging, challenging. The main thing the work in the National Library challenged in that first year there was my patience.

'Well, well,' Bo looked at me quizzically with his steady probing eyes. 'You are very young. There will be other trains to catch.'

'Yes.'

Such as? Which station do those trains they stop at? Where are they bound? Not the station called Department of Irish Folklore, University College Dublin, destination Fulfilment and Happiness in Your Work.

Bo never advised a career in folklore, although he was supervising my PhD in that subject. Like most professors of interesting but impractical subjects in the humanities then, and perhaps now, he avoided the topic of careers and didn't spend much time worrying about the future job prospects of his students. His devotion was to research, his and theirs, to scholarship per se. He loved the subject passionately, believed that there was no task on earth more important than the collection, preservation, and study of Irish folklore. And he succeeded in transmitting this ardour, this passion for learning and research, to almost all his students. As to earning a living, their servants, Luck and Opportunity and Optimism, would have to look after that for them. They'd served Bo well, as it happened. He'd followed his dream, relentlessly, without thought of gain or self-interest, and he had succeeded in earning a living, in getting a good job – he was one of the youngest professors in UCD when he got his chair. Nobody forced the students to go on studying although nobody discouraged them either. How could they? The motives for taking on doctoral students in those days were pure; back then, as far as I know, the departments didn't even get brownie points in the form of credits as a reward for having PhD students, as they do now. On the contrary, they probably earned the envy of their colleagues, which was far from harmless, the universities being staffed almost entirely by clever, pompous, and viciously competitive men, at least 50 per cent of whom were as actively engaged in long-term feuds as poisonous if not as physical as those exercising the Mafia or gangs of drug dealers. But, even so, it was impossible not to feel just a little pride in the fact that many students wanted to go on to doctoral level, under one's supervision. Wasn't it just mildly flattering that one had been such an inspirational teacher that so many got hooked? Almost all! Yes. Almost all Bo's students went on to do MAs and quite a high proportion of them didn't stop at that. On they went to the tenth degree, to do doctorates, even though the prospects of ever getting a job in the subject – Folklore, Ethnology – were as close to nil as made no difference. We are the music makers, we are the dreamers of dreams! They studied and researched and did not look to the future. The future would come and hit them in the face like a gangster, or creep up on them like a hired assassin. Most would survive the assault, slowly recover, and drift out of dream and into reality, until finally the old world of passion, learning and exploration was forgotten, and the new regime became normal, then accepted, then the only good and possible way. For what do we teach our students if not the ability to adapt? What do the legends tell us if not that there is much in life outside our control?

In folk tales, attempts to manipulate the future generally end in failure. Look at the story I was writing about: 'With His Whole Heart'. A bailiff meets the devil. The devil is walking around planning to take anyone who is cursed and offered to him that day. The bailiff figures that he will have something to gain if he teams up with the devil. First they pass a garden. A woman is chasing a pig who is eating the cabbages. 'The devil take you, you pest of a pig!' she cries. The bailiff thinks, great, now I get some fine pork. But the devil says, no. That curse didn't come from the heart so he can't take the pig. At the next cottage a mother is chasing her child who has broken a cup. 'The devil take you, you rascal!' she shouts. Once again the devil rejects the offer, because it was not from the heart. The bailiff, one might think, should begin to get worried. But like most characters in this kind of folk tale he has a short memory and never learns from experience. The next house is the bailiff's own destination. He is issuing an eviction notice to the widow who lives there. 'May the devil take you, bailiff!' she cries, when she sees him coming. 'Aha,' says the devil. 'That curse came from the heart!' And he picks up the bailiff and stuffs him into his black bag and carries him off to hell.

You cannot outwit the devil. You cannot manipulate fate. Look to the legends, Bo enjoined, if you want to learn something about life.

He took his pipe out of his pocket, a packet of tobacco from the desk drawer, and began to fill his pipe. Soon the room was rich with the sweet aroma of tobacco smoke. He looked up, and asked, as an afterthought (although perhaps not; Bo could always think on his feet, and ask the pertinent question at the right moment), 'What about Oliver?'

'We broke up.'

The room was dim, Bo's room, always dim and shadowy as a cave, with its dark books and dark table and window on to a dark atrium filled with gloomy evergreen ferns that never got the sun. I said these words as if they were ordinary – as they are. Three little words. 'I love you' on a journey to 'We broke up.' Or to 'Sorry for your loss.'

Formulae are handy, all right. I could say these three words without emotion. At that moment, I felt none, in the dim, harmonious room, a haven of order and learning. Who would lose control in a room where the dignity of books prevailed, where the love of learning perfumed the air as easily and naturally as if books were wild flowers? The musty spice of old bindings, the leafy richness of Bo's tobacco enhanced the mood. Also I was sitting close to Bo; being close to him physically injected me with confidence, then and always. It was as if his own courage, his self-knowledge, his energy, pulled me into his aura – perhaps that's what charismatic people can do for those who are not charismatic? His body radiated something that threw around me a protective bubble, filled with some nourishing element, psychological oxygen. Under his spell I was reminded that there is more to life than the everyday, more to it than the present, more to it than standard personal relations. There are books. There are stories. There is love of humankind, and research, tales to be collected, books to be written, work to be done. So get on with it.

'We broke up.' A nutshell, enclosing in its neat cup months of quarrels, sulks, lies and heartbreak. Bo got it, of course. You don't need to spell everything out in all the gory detail to sympathetic people.

But even this commonplace formula was a lie. Because Oliver had broken up with me. I would never have left him. I had been in love with him and in many ways he was the right sort of man for me, and I was right for him, at least in my own opinion, which apparently he no longer shared. Both students, both ambitious, both medievalists, and sensible within those limits. It was just that he wanted more than I could give, someone more bright and beautiful and sparkly, and also less personally ambitious – who, unlike me, was probably not going to be a person who would sit beside him for ten hours translating quite boring or wildly incoherent texts from a medieval language to modern English, and then cook a good meal or walk for five miles in the countryside. Although there were, he believed just then, at the breaking-up time, a number of possible candidates for the post whom he planned to try out. He'd mentioned names, and hinted that there were others. A shortlist and a longlist, he seemed to have.

I had applied for the scholarship to Denmark the day after he had broken it off. Always get away, do something new, put water between yourself and the source of the pain. I'd read this piece of advice in a novel by Somerset Maugham and saved it up for a rainy day. Pack your bags and board the next ship to Singapore.

But anyway. I had always wanted to get away. Emigration was the curse of Ireland, in theory, but I yearned for it. Wanderlust infected me, as it had the medieval monks I read about – like them, I longed to get out of Ireland and see the world, to live in some other country, although not for the same reasons. Still, motives are always mixed when it comes to emigration. Oliver had persuaded me to stay when I'd been offered the job in Algeria. And now he was breaking up with me. How could he? Of course he could, had every right to. Love is a gamble. It doesn't come with a ten-year guarantee.

I had to escape. Algeria? Denmark? Anywhere that was not Ireland would do. Though preferably a place where they spoke a language that was not English; countries with their own language are so much more exotic, more entertaining.

Bo was startled.

His eyebrows shot up. He looked me in the eye.

'I am very sorry to hear that!' he said. Such a compassionate tone he had when he said that. He had a lovely voice: deep, expressive. It could sound very cheerful or very encouraging or very serious or very kind. Or very sad, though not often.

'Thank you.'

'I hope you are all right.'

'I'm fine.'

At that moment it was not a lie.

'Well, well …'

He was at a loss, which was unusual for him. He did not know

11

what to say next. But give him five seconds.

'Perhaps we should meet and discuss your plans for Denmark.' He laughed. 'More informally.'

I felt a lightening of the heart such as I had not felt in about a year.

'I wouldn't mind,' I said, in my meek, neutral, UCD student voice.

'I will telephone you. At the library. Would that be all right?'

'Yes.'

It was the only way. I was seldom at home and there was only one phone in the house where I had my bedsitter, a coin box in the hall. No mobile phones or emails in 1978.

DAY 11,985

Autumn sonata

At the October bank holiday weekend Bo and I drove to
Gweedore, in Donegal. Usually at this time of year we went to
Uppsala, in Sweden, to attend the annual meeting and banquet
of the Gustavus Adolphus Academy on 6 November. This was
a gala event, held in the medieval castle, Uppsala Slott: in the
vast cloistered hall, by the light of hundreds of candles, the most
renowned historians and ethnologists of the Nordic countries
gathered to eat, drink and be merry. The women wore evening
frocks, the men *frack*: tails and white tie. Lots of them were
festooned with medals and decorations like characters in stories
by Chekhov. I loved it. The banquet was glamorous and held in
an exquisite setting, and it provided us with an excuse to visit
Sweden and do some Christmas shopping before settling into
Ireland for the winter.

But this year we were not going. Bo had been tired. Two years
ago, in 2001, he had been diagnosed with prostate cancer, and
had had a long course of radiotherapy. The cancer was cured, but
the treatment had aged him and left him tired. In addition there
was a regular round of check-ups, and visits to the consultant
and the doctor. It seemed just too complicated to head off to
Sweden. Instead I had committed to giving a workshop in
creative writing in Acadamh Ghaoth Dobhair, with Micheál Ó
Conghaile, a friend, writer and publisher, from Connemara. I
persuaded Bo to come with me. We were going to spend a day in

Gweedore, and then drive over to Fanad, to the old cottage that had belonged to my parents. I liked to visit it once a year or so.

We were both very happy, in celebratory mood. Bo had had his six-month cancer check-up three weeks earlier, and just yesterday had got the news that all was well, he was cancer-free. The check-ups were always worrying, the telephone calls confirming that everything was okay a joy and a great relief. Off the hook for another six months.

It was a fine day. Crisp air, light breeze, the splendid leaves performing their giddy dance of death: seductive, endlessly entertaining. We decided to get going and be well out on the road before stopping for lunch, since our aim was to drive in daylight as much as possible. We had an appointment to meet Micheál for dinner in Na Cúirteanna, the hotel in Gweedore, at eight that evening. I drove – Bo had stopped driving four years ago after he had a crash in his little blue Micra, outside Ballyferriter, in Kerry. He had believed, he often told me, that he was going to die then. Blinded by the low strong sunlight of late September, he had swerved on to the wrong side of the road and collided with an oncoming car. Luckily the driver of that car had slowed to a standstill, and Bo was also driving slowly. The airbag activated and almost smothered him – cracking a rib – and the car began to fill with smoke. But the driver of the other car got him out and phoned the ambulance. He was brought to Tralee General Hospital, where he was examined in A&E, and discharged at 1 a.m. He was completely alone – I was in Dublin and did not know about this accident. He knew nobody in Tralee. He asked if he could stay on his trolley until the trains started running in the morning and his request was acceded to. Early in the morning he got a taxi to the station and took the first train back to Dublin.

I was teaching a creative writing class that morning, when Terry, a friend of mine from Dunquin, rang. He said a blue car that looked a bit like Bo's had been involved in a crash outside Ballyferriter and asked if we were all right. I assured her that we were and she said, 'Oh it was probably somebody else's car.' Some minutes later Bo telephoned me and told me the whole story.

Two days later a doctor from Tralee Hospital rang and said the initial diagnosis – that Bo was uninjured – wasn't correct. Further examination of the X-rays showed he had fractured a rib. He was advised to go to a hospital in Dublin.

This was one of Bo's encounters with real danger, and one of our first encounters with the small failures that inevitably occur in hospitals. That had been a small mistake, with no serious consequences. Sometimes you can be lucky.

The hotel in Gweedore was not one I was familiar with. It is in a hollow niche at the side of the road on a hillside overlooking the Clady river, and the mountains, and Errigal – none of which you can see in the dark. But it is on the main road, and well signposted, so even in the pitch-black night, we found it easily.

The lobby was full of wedding guests. They milled around, drinking coffee and champagne from a carnivalesque chocolate trolley perched beside the reception desk. Women and girls dressed in satin and silk dresses, pink and yellow and blue, tottered on heels six inches high, with elaborate hair styles and little fascinators – the wedding uniform down the country, which is unlike anything anyone ever wears otherwise. Like tropical insects, dragonflies, hummingbirds, butterflies from the Antipodes, they fluttered all over the lobby. We, coming in from the wilderness outside, smelling of car and rain, in our tweedy work clothes, with our shabby bags, our laptops, felt like aliens from another planet in the midst of these bright satiny creatures.

Micheál phoned the room minutes after we arrived and we met him, as planned, at eight o'clock. When we got to the lobby all the wedding guests had vanished, and all that remained was the white wrought-iron stall with its jars of old-fashioned sweets. '*Tá said imithe isteach chun dinnéara, is dócha,*' Mícheál said.

We had a very good dinner, starting with a seafood plate, in a small, deserted dining room. 'All the other guests are at the wedding,' Micheál said, observing the empty tables surrounding us. What did we talk about? General things, and the workshop we would do tomorrow. As usual Micheál was low-key and reassuring. Although he is a prolific writer and editor and runs one of the longest-surviving and most successful Irish language publishing houses in Ireland, he never seems harassed or worried, and takes life calmly.

One topic we discussed was an Irish language writing workshop I had done with Micheál, and another writer – maybe Alan Titley; neither of us could remember – four or five years before. This workshop took place over a weekend in Connemara. A stunningly picturesque place, an island, and the weather was lovely. I had evolved a particular way of handling these one-day or weekend workshops – I liked to ask students to do some 'out of the box' writing exercises, to discuss aspects of writing (point of view, power of memory, character) and so on, and then move on to review their own work. I had organised a schedule for the workshopping part of the programme – we would review four students per session, let us say. In my workshops, I like everyone to have read and considered all the submitted scripts in advance. I ask students being workshopped to read the first page of their story, or whatever it is, and summarise the rest to remind us of it. Then we review it. I have abandoned the practice whereby each writer reads their entire script aloud in the workshop. While this convention has advantages – the major one being that everyone definitely hears the story even if they haven't bothered to read it in advance – it takes up a huge amount of precious class time, which I believed then to outweigh the advantages. Anyway, we proceeded. My first very easy exercise is one that works very well almost always – describe a room that meant a lot to you as a child. People did the exercise and then, as usual, I asked if anyone would like to share their piece with us. One of the participants, a pleasant, round-faced man wearing spectacles, put up his hand. He read his piece, and then spoke at great length about his father.

What he had to say was extremely interesting. At first. But soon I, and the other facilitator, realised what was happening – a not uncommon occurrence at workshops: one lively person, who is entertaining and extrovert, takes over. Initially he or she is a delight. But soon that participant is talking far too much. Sometimes this person uses the workshop setting as a sort of forum in which to tell the story of his life, as a place for talk therapy. I know these people do not set out consciously to do this; I see it as a sign of their loneliness, and no doubt they do it because they don't have the opportunity to express themselves and tell their story to an understanding, sympathetic audience often enough.

Sympathising with these people, who can provoke perfectly understandable resentment among some or all of their classmates, the less charitable among them who will quickly classify them as loudmouths, makes it difficult to find a way of stopping them. I find it hard to step in and staunch the flow. I believe I tried, and succeeded up to a point, by moving on to the next item on my plan. The dominance of this speaker was one factor that precipitated the events that followed.

Who participated in the workshop? A mixture of people, some from the locality, some from further afield. Several were published writers. That did not mean that they had nothing to learn. Everyone has plenty to learn, always. Writers in Irish often write with the complete spontaneity that writers in English – schooled, now at creative writing classes and in competition with millions of other writers – can lack. They can write with a disregard for artistic discipline that would be unusual among English language writers. The results can be refreshing, original and good. As Theo Dorgan said, launching a translation of Irish short stories edited by Brian Ó Conchubhair and published by Cló Iar-Chonnachta, Micheál's company, about a year before,

'All these writers are nuts. Even the famously sane Éilís Ní Dhuibhne is nuts.' (I paraphrase. I took it as a compliment, which is how it was intended – although my story was very sane, in that anthology.) There is some truth in what Theo said. The stories were more varied, more wild, took more chances – also, more contrived, in some cases, taking the form of unconvincing realism – than any contemporary collection of stories in English could be. Some Irish male writers write what reads to me as soft porn – very old-fashioned fantasies about sexual encounters with beautiful women in unlikely situations, which are probably a reaction to the puritanism of Irish language literature in the early twentieth century. To criticise writing in Irish is not popular, but it seems to me that quite a few Irish language writers would benefit from creative writing classes.

The majority of fiction writers in Irish are men – this has always been the case. For instance, during the twentieth century about 250 novels in the Irish language were published, and only 10 of those were written by women. Sometimes very sweetly, sometimes in ways that are less pleasant, male writers can be defensive, competitive and arrogant. Arrogant women writers are not unheard of, but they're a rare breed.

While one man in that particular workshop talked far too much, another man in that group was silent. For hours he said absolutely nothing. Then, at about three o'clock on Saturday afternoon he stood up and walked out of the room, slamming the door behind him. He did not come back.

I reminded Micheál of this incident.

'Did I ever tell you what happened later?' Micheál asked.

He'd received a solicitor's letter from the workshop participant. The man complained that the workshop had not delivered on what was promised in the description he had received. He was threatening to sue the organiser – Micheál – for damages.

Bo, Micheál and I laughed heartily. This was the first time I had heard of anyone suing because a creative writing workshop was not to their liking. I should add that this workshop was free to participants – their travel, accommodation and tuition, all free. It was funded by some state organisation.

Micheál smiled and said at the time it wasn't funny. It is never nice to receive a solicitor's letter.

'So we have a new yardstick with which to measure the success of a writing workshop. Nobody walked out.'

'Nobody sent a solicitor's letter.'

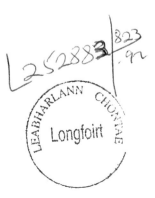

Behind the scenes at the National Library

That May, when Bo fell in love with me – I had been half in love with him for years – I had spent three hundred days working in a big, dreary, untidy room at the back of the National Library on Kildare Street. This office could not have been more different from the library's splendid domed reading room where uniformed attendants, like waiters in an exclusive hotel or gentlemen's club, glided about as if on slippered wheels delivering books to the readers with a polite nod of the head, the merest hint of a bow. The readers thus honoured – a motley assortment of genuine scholars, harmless (and not so harmless) eccentrics, and people sheltering from the rain – sat comfortably at polished tables, their books and faces illuminated by reading lamps with sweet green shades.

The room where I worked had big, steel Anglepoise lamps on the desks, and one bare bulb hanging from the ceiling. It had once been the Ladies' Reading Room. Although it had probably been tidier in the days when it was open to the female public, it looked as if it had been designed purposely to put the Lady Readers off books for life. It was never properly heated, never got the sun, and the grey air that always hung between the drab walls felt damp and discouraging. Two dirty windows with peeling painted frames faced north on to a grubby back lane, at the end of which was Nassau Street, one of Dublin's more stiff and forbidding streets, and the high wall and dark spiked railings that enclosed Trinity College.

It was the kind of room that made your heart sink when you walked into it. This is where I am to work? After all my hard studying?

In those days graduates had a sense of entitlement, and believed that study and good results should lead swiftly to good jobs. And in fact a good degree usually did lead to a job that was well paid and permanent, the sort of job that is almost impossible to get in the twenty-first century in Ireland. It was 1976. Free university education had started at the end of the 1960s but the take-up was still small. Hardly anyone in the country had a degree, still less the class of degree you needed to get a job in the National Library.

Oh, such a lovely place to work! Aren't you lucky?

I spent the year cataloguing new books and seventeenth-century pamphlets.

The pamphlets were the good news – although their titles usually included the words 'Bad News from Ireland'. They were dusty, yellowed, lacking illustrations. The contents were long-winded rants about political events in the seventeenth century. But you were not supposed to read the contents anyway, a rule that was a blessing in the case of the pamphlets. Did anyone ever read them? Even in the seventeenth century? As a librarian you were supposed to count the pages, measure the dimensions of the pamphlet, and read the title page, noting all the details of publication. The pamphlet titles were almost as long as the contents in some instances. The art of the snappy hook was not known in the seventeenth century:

The latest and truest nevves from Ireland; or, A true relation of the happy victory obtained against the rebels before Droheda: and how the Earle of Ormond Sir Charles Coote, and Sir Simon Harecourt sallying out of Dublin to

Donshoglen with two thousand souldiers; slew two hundred rebels, and but 5. of them slain: related in a letter from a privy councellor in Dublin, to Master Fenton Parsons of Lincolns-Inne, Feb 26. 1641. Whereunto is added another relation of an overthrow given them by Sir Henry Tichbourne, being related in a letter to Sir Robert King Knight, Feb 27. 1641 .../

or

A discoverie of the hellish plot against divers particular of the nobility of the kingdome of England: Also the papists gunpowder-plot, brought to light. With the copie of a letter sent from a noble-man in Ireland, to Colonel Lunsford. Jan. 11. 1642. Shewing, in a most true and reall relation, the manner how this hellish plot was laid, and how these noble pillars of Protestant-religion, the Earl of Cork, the Earl of Kildare, and the valourous Lord Iones, should have been blown up. As also, hovv they intended to burn dovvn the citie of Dublin with wild-fire, and how they were beaten back by the lord chief-justices in the castles.

The contemporary publications were less challenging to catalogue but much easier to read. Even though you weren't supposed to read books at work, a perk was that you could borrow them for reading at home. Which I did. Novels by John McGahern, Terence de Vere White, Benedict Kiely, Iris Murdoch. Or the new women writers who were just starting their careers and getting published in slim paperbacks: Maeve Kelly or Ita Daly or Emma Cooke.

Some aspects of the job, however, were very enjoyable. The young Assistant Keepers were on duty for one day a week, and one night. When on duty you sat behind a big desk in the Librarian's Office, or LO. Originally the LO had been the Director's Office, and as such is the setting for the scene in *Ulysses* in which Stephen talks to the Librarian.

This famous room was just off the Reading Room, but readers had little or no access to it – the Library Assistants, mostly men, who manned the big counter, and some of whom had worked in the library for decades, could handle almost every enquiry themselves. And even when they couldn't, it was a matter of pride with them to keep readers well away from the Assistant Keepers, young people, increasingly young women like me, whom they regarded with friendly contempt. So while on duty we were left in relative peace. Our job was to answer telephone queries and letters of enquiry, and take orders for photocopying – a new technology for the library, with which it was very very slowly coming to terms, and a service that was so expensive and cumbersome that not many readers could avail of it. The Assistant Keepers were enjoined to do minimal research on behalf of enquirers, who should be pointed in the right direction and encouraged to find things out for themselves. Our guideline was the mantra, coined by the Director, 'A helpful librarian is a bad librarian.' The queries could relate to anything. Can you advise me on books about the Battle of Clontarf? I am researching the Cork writer, Margaret O'Leary. Any help you can give me will be appreciated. Have you got a photograph of the Famine? Have you got a photograph of St Patrick/St Bridget/Niall of the Nine Hostages?

But most of the queries related to genealogy. The hunt for roots was relentless. My great-great-grandfather left Cork in 1847. Can you help me find information about him? My great-grandmother, Catherine Ann Doherty, came from Donegal in 1856. I would like to research her ancestry. Can you please send me information about her parents and grandparents?

Although the instruction was to give general rather than specific information to enquirers, in practice how one dealt with these queries as Librarian on Duty was entirely up to oneself. I was a 'bad librarian' in more ways than one. For entirely selfish reasons I tried to answer the readers' questions, doing whatever research was necessary, and resisting the temptation to remind the innumerable enquirers in search of photographs of medieval kings or early Christian saints that photography was not invented until the 1840s and so photographs of fifth-century saints were unlikely to be in stock. I contented myself with mild bureaucratic diplomacy, always most satisfactory to the bureaucrat who composes it: 'I regret to inform you that we do not have a photograph of Brian Boru in our holdings. However, a pen and ink illustration is reproduced in *An Leabharlann*, Vol. XII, p. 46. We can supply a photocopy of this, at a cost of fifty pence plus postage and packing.'

The genealogical queries were glanced at, sighed over or laughed at, and then despatched in fat bundles to the Genealogical Office, the busiest section of the Library, located in a tower in Dublin Castle.

When on duty you communicated with readers on the telephone or by letter, or more rarely in person. You carried out research on a multitude of topics, you learnt how to find sources in the Library, and got a sense of its depth and usefulness. You got the odd laugh, and an occasional invitation to go on a date. Usually these approaches were made when you were on night duty, the green-shaded lamps glowing in the dimness like candles, the only sounds the whisper of pages being turned, a soft voice murmuring goodbye as a reader slipped gently into the night. At night, the Library felt exactly as it must have at the start of the century. It was easy to imagine that Joyce was reading by the gaslight, or that bureaucrats with vivid faces were slipping down to the steps to have a smoke and to exchange polite meaningless words, or discuss their dreams of an armed rebellion.

I had limited access to the duty desk – as a new recruit, I was considered too inexperienced to deal with its challenges, except in cases of emergency, such as, for instance, when the real Librarian On Duty was on her tea break, or out to lunch.

'It gets easier as you get used to it,' Maurice, the Assistant Keeper Grade One, who supervised the Assistant Keepers Grade

Two, said. 'The first two years are the hardest.'

It's what they say about widowhood.

Most of the time I catalogued the pamphlets and the books. That was not too bad. At least I was sitting down, and there were moments of brightness. Finding the appropriate subject heading demanded a certain ingenuity.

But there was much duller work going on. And for at least half the year, that year in the library, I did it. This work was called 'Checking the Booksellers' Catalogues'.

The National Library's original acquisitions policy had been to collect books and publications and manuscripts of Irish interest, as well as literature of international importance. But from the early 1970s, it collected only books of Irish interest.

The books were acquired in the following way. Booksellers, who had become aware of the library's policy, began to specialise in buying up books of Irish interest, old and new. Every week, sometimes more often, a bookseller's catalogue would arrive on Maurice's desk in the Cataloguing Room. These catalogues were amateurish publications, sometimes printed, sometimes typed lists that had been photocopied and bound with staples. Typically they would offer for sale five or six hundred books, of diverse nature, but all 'of Irish interest'. Library staff would then identify which ones were not in the collection, and buy them.

Maurice would have a look at the bookseller's catalogue when it arrived. Sitting at his desk by the window, he would hum and haw and tick off the books he suspected we did not have – quite a lot of them. His instinct, or knowledge, was good, but – quite sensibly – he erred on the side of caution and ticked many books which were, in fact, in the collection.

The catalogue was then ripped apart and sections given to the five or six Assistant Keepers. It was up to us to check the marked books against the two main catalogues: if a book was not listed in the library's collection, it would be bought. By this means gaps were filled and the National Library's collection of books of Irish interest up to the late 1970s is very comprehensive.

But the work of looking up title after title in the catalogue for days on end was tedious in the extreme. As the readers who adore the National Library know, it is great fun to search for three or four books in the catalogue of a great library – the Guard Books are especially engaging, because you often see names and titles that fascinate you as you check for a particular item. But standing at the Guard Book stand, looking up two hundred titles, one after the other, is not enjoyable. The only skill required was a knowledge of the alphabet and basic literacy. I had an MPhil in Medieval Studies. I was writing a doctoral thesis. I was a writer of short stories. Like many young people, I had quite a high opinion of my talents and abilities. The other Assistant Keepers had first-class honours in subjects like Latin or English or History.

'It is a bit boring,' Maurice admitted. As a Grade One, he didn't have to check titles himself. 'It's the sort of work we should get temporary staff to do. Married women,' he intoned, and laughed drily.

Everyone agreed. But of course! This was the kind of menial work married women could do in their spare time, for pin money, when their children had gone to school. The library didn't employ temporary or part-time staff back then. Or married women, in any capacity except that of cleaning lady, although I didn't notice this at the time – we always have our blind spots.

This was the kind of work that a computer could do in seconds – and did, when computers finally arrived in the National Library in the late 1980s.

And yet there were several positive aspects to working in the National Library in the 1970s, principally the interesting workmates and 'the stacks'. The stacks were the old iron bookshelves that stretched from the ground floor over three or four storeys to the roof. On the shelves over a million books were lined up neatly, according to subject. Poetry, fiction, history, geography, ethnology, women. It was a vast, hushed, magical place unlike anything I have ever encountered, before or since. Walking through the stacks was inspiring and uplifting, as if the books, some dating back three or four centuries, were singing a gentle ancient incantation: Read me, read me, read me! For me, the stacks was a space as spiritual in atmosphere as a cathedral, a precious monument, not to the glory of God but for the glory of knowledge, literature and the human imagination. My religion, even then – perhaps especially back then.

But in many ways I was totally unsuited for much of the work, which seemed to me mechanical and repetitive. I was not neat and orderly; I had no talent for the kind of librarianship then practised. It was neither creative nor intellectually challenging. All this changed in later years and now the National Library has been transformed. But in 1978, the decision that many kind friends saw as rash was the right one for me. I had to get out of the library.

DAY 11,989

The end of the rainbow

The Saturday workshop in Acadamh Ghaoth Dobhair was successful and enjoyable. As in the best creative writing workshops, the atmosphere was friendly and industrious. I was above all impressed by the fluent mellifluous Irish of the eight or nine participants, and some of them had composed excellent poems or stories. The day passed quickly, and on Sunday Bo and I left Gweedore and drove east to the cottage on Lough Swilly.

It's an old house, dating from the eighteenth century, owned by my parents during the last decades of their lives, and now shared by me, my brother and my sister. Nestling among big old trees in a large garden, with the hills behind and the sea in front, it must have looked really beautiful when its roof was thatched, but even with grey slates it has a hospitable appearance. Everything was in fine shape – the grass in the garden was cut, the fire set on the hearth. My brother Donagh (one of the kindest, wisest and most entertaining people I know) and his lovely wife, Linda, had hung some pictures on the walls – reproductions of paintings by Monet, Van Gogh, Jack B. Yeats. Bo and I were both pleased by the pictures, which were predictable but which the house needed. We unpacked the car – all our stuff, out again, with added bags of food. After lunch, Bo lay down for a nap and I went for a walk on the beach – the walk I have so often taken with him, but that he hasn't been able to do for two years now, because of pain in his back.

The beach – Stocker Beach, Warden Strand, an Trá Bán, Portsalon strand; *kärt barn har många namn*, a beloved child has many names – is a few miles long. It stretches in a shallow crescent from the foot of the Knockalla hills to the cliffs at Portsalon – the last wide bay in Lough Swilly, facing the open sea which looks very 'North Atlantic' at this place, cold and vast, stretching from Donegal to the Arctic. The sea is often rough, and so it was today. Great waves broke on the sand; the sea roared, its voice like that of angry lions or of heavy traffic pounding along a motorway.

The beach is magnificent, a fine sandy beach that is sometimes golden, sometimes russet. It's bisected by a river – Warden Burn – about half a kilometre from the place where you enter through the sloping dunes, the silvery green marram grass spouting from the sand. You used to have to wade through this river to cross it. Bo always hated doing that, even in summer when the water level was low. He didn't like taking off his shoes and socks, and putting them back on again at the other side, and he never felt confident on uneven surfaces – for some years, his toes felt numb sometimes, and he didn't trust his sense of balance. And even in summer, Warden Burn is cold. That meant that Bo seldom walked the full length of the beach – perhaps three miles or so. In 2011 however, the county council thoughtfully bridged the river, as close to the landward side of the beach as they could, since near the sea it changed course constantly. The following winter the bridge caved in under pressure from storms and when we were last in Donegal in late May it was unusable. The burn was now in flood, its voice up, its waters swollen and rushing fast towards the ocean. Impossible to wade through. But I walked up towards the land and – hey presto! – the bridge was there, rebuilt, allowing easy access to the other bank. Indeed, I met three or four groups, mostly families or couples, with their dogs, all 'walking the beach'.

I walked a few kilometres, as far as the next burn, just before the cove of Portsalon itself, and then returned. The sea was still splendidly rough and loud, lashing in on the sand – Emily Brontë would have loved it. But a few hundred yards out, it looked smooth as a mirror, and bobbing about on the lake of calm water were two large birds. Not seagulls, not cormorants. Grebes? They swam about looking as if the great wide bay was under their exclusive command, as if they had a magical druidic power to calm a section of the stormy ocean, the way a farmer moulds a field out of mountainside or forest.

Clouds scudded across the iron sea as I was halfway back, but it rained only for a minute. Then a magnificent rainbow appeared. I photographed it with both my camera and my phone, and sent the snap to my sister Síle with the text, *End of the rainbow.*

Later – dinner, then Bo and I sat down by the fire to enjoy the Sunday night episode of *Downton Abbey*. To our disappointment, we couldn't get it, and when I phoned my brother he said there was a problem with the television set and it wasn't receiving that channel any more. Drat! We were both irritated. Such minor things do irritate you – when life is normal, when life is at its best. We played Scrabble instead. I won by quite a wide margin and Bo laughed. The page with our score that night is still in the box. But he wasn't trying very hard and my easy victory puzzled me. Bo always loved to win a game. This wasn't like him. I guessed the pain in his back was very bad, or that he felt unusually tired, and my heart sank.

There was a loneliness in the cottage that night. Perhaps the ghosts of my parents hovered? For Bo, if not for me. Because the next day he wanted to go to their grave, in the small churchyard in Glenvar overlooking Lough Swilly. We visited it briefly, in driving rain. I never visited graves – then. I didn't see the point. But he did.

We slept in the big bed in the room at the back. Our room, traditionally – we have always slept there, ever since my parents got the cottage. Bo complained of the cold, and the room was freezing – even though the central heating was on it did little more than take the bite out of the chill in that room, with its three exterior stone walls, in this wintry weather. Next morning Bo said he hadn't slept well. So we decided to move to the room in the middle, which adjoined the kitchen. It was warmer there, although we had to sleep in single beds, which Bo hated. Somehow the cosiness of the marital bed was very important to him – it was more important to him than to me, or to most people of his age, or even my age, as far as I have noticed. Even in hotels, where sometimes we were given rooms with adjoining twin beds, Bo seemed to feel abandoned even though I often slept better. He, however, had the great gift of being able to fall asleep as soon as he had read for fifteen minutes and turned out the light, and usually he slept peacefully till morning. *Ett rent samvete är den besta huvudkudden*, a clear conscience, he claimed, is the best pillow. Sometimes I could lie awake for hours, waiting for sleep to come, and I often woke at four in the morning. Bo would be sleeping like a newborn baby. I often put my hand to his chest to check that he was breathing, whereupon he would wake up for a second and say impatiently, 'Yes, yes, I am still alive.' And then fall fast asleep again.

We stayed in Magherawarden for Monday and Tuesday. The days followed the same routine. In the morning, I wrote – I was preparing a speech for a book launch on that Thursday, 31 October, Halloween, and a short presentation that I was going to give at the concert in aid of the National Folklore Collection, which would take place on the same night. Bo wrote in the small room – what was he writing? I can't remember. Probably he was working on the introduction to a second selection of stories by Peig Sayers, stories for which sound recordings survive. He went for a walk, on both mornings, not to the beach but up the boreen past Knockalla Caravan Park, which is not far from the cottage, and along there – a leafy ramble; it pleased him that he could do this walk without difficulty, and, smiling in delight, he reported that his back was not aching. Bo had a true capacity for happiness; he was naturally cheerful, and tiny pleasures, such as this, lifted his spirits enormously.

On the Monday afternoon, I did the beach walk again, and on one of those days we drove, at Bo's request, down to Fanad lighthouse, along the small roads of the peninsula, which wend their way dreamily between a landscape of hills and drumlins and lakes and the sea: a landscape that looks like a picture in a particularly beautiful children's book. This part of Donegal, between Mulroy Bay and Lough Swilly, is not very well known but it is one of the most exquisite places on earth. We shopped a little in the local store, the Blueberry – and we tried to find some information in the tiny local museum they have upstairs there. Some question we had about the locality – about megalithic remains, dolmens, in the area. Just a few weeks previously we had visited Lough Gur, in County Limerick, which is rich in ancient archaeological artefacts and which has been inhabited for four or five thousand years, and were wondering if this part of Donegal had an early history of settlement, or if it had been settled later? The museum did not hold the answer and in fact I still don't know, since very soon such questions were far from the forefront of my mind.

Summer in Dunquin

Bo knew Oliver, my boyfriend, my fiancé, because while I was a student on the MPhil programme in Medieval Studies, and Bo's student, Oliver and I were one of those college couples you can see on any campus in the world. Glued together from morning till night. We studied together, we ate together, we walked home together. Mean students joked that we went to the loo together. When you are young and in love you want to be with the beloved all the time, and, if you are a student, you can do this. It's natural. But I'm not sure if it is good. The self becomes subsumed in the other – there is no boundary, no sense of being a separate person. Then, if things do not work out, the shock is terrible.

Actually, although we seemed to be glued together, we were apart for quite a lot of time, because I tutored in Old English for two or three hours a week, and I also worked as a 'Trainee Cataloguer', indexing folklore manuscripts, in the Folklore Archive in UCD for fifteen hours – a job, as it were, three days a week. On my cataloguing mornings, Oliver would call in to the archive and collect me at lunchtime. Very tall and striking in his smart casual clothes, he was a familiar figure on the corridor of the Department of Irish Folklore.

It is an enchanting corridor, unlike anywhere else in Belfield, hung with big paintings on Irish ethnographical themes – *The Pattern at Glendalough*, *The Eviction*, *Donnybrook Fair*. This richly-coloured, evocative passage linked the front office to the manuscript archive, where the oral tradition of Ireland, transcribed, handwritten, was stored in hundreds of brown leather volumes. It's all too easy to wax sentimental about anything with the word 'Folklore' in it. But the Department of Irish Folklore was like an Aladdin's cave, full of rich colours and beautiful manuscripts and books, full of curious objects – the big black Ediphone machines (the earliest sound recorders), various types of St Brigid's Cross. It was exotic and authentic, natural and hi-tech, artistic and scientific, all at the same time. In the grey utilitarian setting of Belfield, it glowed like a precious jewel. And it was a secret, separate from the rest of the Arts Block, down at the back of the building. Hardly anyone seemed to know it existed.

Over this kingdom Bo presided; it was entirely in keeping with the mood of the Department of Irish Folklore that its director should sail over the sea from the land of the Vikings, that he should speak Irish and English with a strong foreign accent, that he should bring skills and ideas and standards from the Nordic world to this little kingdom down at the back of Belfield.

Bo saw Oliver tramping down the magical corridor to collect me every Monday, Tuesday and Wednesday during term time. But he got to know him better during the final summer of my MPhil.

This is how it happened.

Bo was my thesis supervisor. But not much supervision had been carried out during the year, for reasons unknown to me, and about which I did not enquire. Students were very passive in those days. At the best of times supervision was a bit haphazard. Even teaching could be random. When I was an undergraduate in the English department, it was not unusual for some lecturers simply not to turn up for small classes – a group of ten or so students or so would hang around outside the lecturer's room for half an hour, and then simply go away. We never thought of complaining. Who would you complain to?

So I simply accepted that Bo had not had time to meet me to

34

discuss the progress of my thesis. I was in any case fully occupied with my trainee cataloguing, and my classes and homework in Old Irish, which I was taking as a second subject in the MPhil and which took up an inordinate proportion of my time. Old Irish is a very hard language! The MPhil in Medieval Studies was a challenging degree. In addition, Bo had assigned another lecturer, Dáithí Ó hOgáin, to check my translations of stories from Irish (modern Irish, that is) to English. That had been systematic enough. It was easy to translate the tales and Dáithí had gone over my work with me regularly. But as the summer term drew to its close I was getting a bit panicky about the thesis. I had a thick wad of translated stories, but not much in the way of analysis. The chapters that I had written had been read by nobody but myself and the deadline was approaching. On 1 September fifty thousand words would have to be handed in, typed and bound, in three copies.

At the last minute, when term was over, Bo took action. He invited me to his house in the country for a week of intensive supervision. Oliver was also invited, since as far as Bo could see, he and I were inseparable. Another doctoral student, a girl called Mandy, completed the party.

Bo, Mandy and I were driven to Kerry by one of the full-time collectors, Con Breslin, in Con's car, a Cortina. Oliver was to come later, on the bus. Bo didn't drive at that stage and Con acted as his chauffeur once or twice a year, at Easter, when the folklore students carried out fieldwork in the country, and at the beginning and end of the summer, which Bo spent collecting and writing about folklore in his house in Dunquin, near Dingle in County Kerry.

Mandy and I sat in the back, Bo in the passenger seat. Mandy came from Cheshire. She was writing a doctoral thesis about T.W. Thompson.

'Have you heard of him?'

'The name rings a bell,' I lied.

Bo looked over his shoulder. 'He collected gypsy stories, in

England. He's quite important.'

'There you are!' Mandy rolled her eyes. 'He's quite important.'

'And he'll be very important by the time you're finished with him,' Con said. 'If you ever are.'

Bo lit a cigarette and opened his window, but the car filled with smoke anyway.

'I hope this isn't bothering you, girls,' he said.

'Oh no.' Nothing ever bothered me.

'It's getting in my eyes,' Mandy squeaked.

'I'm sorry! Are you suffering?'

'It's very bad for you, smoking.'

'Would you like one yourself?'

'Not at the moment, thank you.'

Mandy was on the plump side. She had a soft, smooth complexion, light brown wavy hair, and very pleasant features: a little retroussé nose, big blue eyes, a wide, generous mouth. Her good looks, combined with her Englishness and her prosperous background, gave her an air of self-confidence that I knew I would never have.

Mandy talked a lot about herself, in the car on the way down, and when we got to the summer house. She talked about herself all the time. Her parents lived in a big rectory, as far as I could gather – but I didn't think her father was a rector; perhaps he was just one of those rich men you read about in Nancy Mitford novels, whose money was inherited, one of those men who didn't have to work for a living. Her mother was stunningly beautiful and amazingly intelligent but used her brilliance to do crossword puzzles. She also rode horses regularly.

All this we found out before we got to Dingle.

Woodlands, gates, avenues. Coats of arms hanging in the stone hall. That's what I saw, as I listened, nodded, told nothing about my own life – I felt fully alive in college, but at home I was, as it were, crouched in the corner of the hall, with my bags packed, like a refugee preparing to escape. My real life hadn't started, I didn't know what it would be like. There was no point in describing the transitory state I was in – the home of my childhood and adolescence was a nest to which I didn't belong, it seemed to me. It was just a temporary shelter, of which I was ashamed, and had no intention of describing to anyone. A butterfly might as well describe the interior of its cocoon, or a baby the walls of the womb. So I listened to Mandy babbling on, to Con's grunts, to Bo's occasional ironic comments, and watched Ireland rolling by.

In those days, the road to west Kerry went right through all the towns and villages between Dublin and Dingle – you had to drive along the main streets of little towns like Monasterevin, Newbridge, Mountrath, Moneygall, Toomevara, and big ones, like Naas, Portlaoise, Roscrea, Nenagh, Limerick, Tralee. We set off on Monday morning; there was not much traffic. The countryside was at its most lush, the fields green like wet emeralds, fat cows chewing the cud under trees heavy with rich, thick leaves. Alder and meadowsweet. Foxgloves, purple vetch, ox-eye daisies and dozens of other wild flowers burgeoning in the hedgerows along the two-lane road, not yet known as the N7. Roads still had proper names: the Naas Road, turning into the Limerick Road when you got through Naas. Country towns were still vibrant, full of people and shops and little businesses. Doused in syrupy July sunshine, they looked not asleep or dead – as they all too often look these days – but as if they were just taking the morning off to sunbathe. With confidence, in businesslike fashion, the old, dusty shop windows displayed their wares – flowery blouses and high-heeled shoes, aprons, cans of paint and spades and sweeping brushes, packets of cornflakes: hardware stores and grocery shops and haberdasheries. Newsagents. Butchers. Hairdressers with witty names: Golden Scissors. Snips. A Cut Above. Supermarkets existed – Dunnes had opened in Cornelscourt in 1966 – but shopping centres were extremely rare. Down the country, people still came to Main Street to do the big shop.

There weren't many cafes or restaurants in the towns, though, big or small. Plenty of chip shops. Prim old hotels, for solicitors and doctors and parish priests, with roses in the porch, lace curtains on the elegant, shining windows. A smell of whisky.

A superabundance of pubs, naturally.

We stopped in Portlaoise, for coffee in a pub, the sort of pub where you could get coffee – one that had been done up recently, with plastic soft seats, and Formica-topped tables. Con ordered a pint of Guinness and a chaser, Bo and Mandy and I coffees. Nescafé.

'Would you like a scone?'

Bo always ate something with his cup of coffee. And smoked a cigarette afterwards.

'I'd love one!'

'No, thanks.' That was me.

'That's how you're so slim,' Mandy said.

'Yes,' I said. 'I starve.'

You could win a few Brownie points if you said that, which cancelled out the ones you lost for being slim and not eating a scone, dripping with butter and finished with a dollop of strawberry jam. Nobody wants to hear that you can eat anything and stay skinny. And in my case, that wasn't true. I had a good figure because I watched my diet like a hawk. I had watched it for so long that I no longer felt hungry, ever, and occasionally regretted the loss of that sensation, with which I had been extremely familiar in childhood – though not in a bad way. I used to feel hungry for my dinner, and full, satisfied and bouncing with energy, even intellectual energy, when I had eaten. But I hadn't felt like that since I was seventeen, and discovered dieting.

We stopped again in Nenagh. Con parked on the side of the main street, and we trooped into a hotel, grey stone, ivy-covered, pink roses rambling around the door. In the dining room the tables were covered with white linen cloths, the silver sparkled and so did the glasses. There was a silver bud vase containing two red carnations in the centre of the table. A smell of roasting meat, the tinkle of clinking glass and silver, a hum of low voices conversing quietly across an expanse of starched linen. Oxtail soup, roast pork with apple sauce, roast potatoes, cabbage and carrots.

Con had a pint of stout, Bo a glass of Carlsberg, Mandy and I drank water. I drew the line at apple pie or trifle, and so did Con, who excused himself and said he'd see us back at the car. Bo took the pie and Mandy the trifle.

'Life's too short.' She picked a fat cherry from the bottom of the dish, and licked custard and cream from a thick spoon. Bo smiled appreciatively. 'Anyway I'm going to Weight Watchers when I get back to Dublin.'

Finally, after several more coffee breaks, we arrived in Dingle, the small fishing village built on a hill sliding down into the bay.

'I need to do some shopping –' Bo's face was anxious – 'otherwise we'll *all* starve.'

His Swedish accent never disappeared when he spoke English, but it became more pronounced when he was anxious.

Mandy glanced at me and we nodded in female complicity.

'We'll give you a hand,' Mandy offered.

'That would be very helpful!' His smile came back.

'See yez back at the car,' said Con, and hurried through a red door in a garden wall, quick as an *Alice in Wonderland* rabbit.

The house in Dunquin is a small dormer bungalow, although bungalow is a word that conveys the wrong impression entirely. It's a modern cottage, with a nicely designed interior – wooden ceilings and a tiled stone floor, carefully selected country furniture, a kind of modernist country design that was rare in Ireland in 1976. Everyone assumed it had a Scandinavian look, but the house was designed by a German architect, and did not look particularly Scandinavian at all, although it had some Swedish touches in the form of textiles and wall hangings. The cutlery and utensils had come from Sweden, and the bed linen and tablecloth, a wonderfully bright white oilcloth with a huge green and black pattern, which lifted the mood of the house, like a child's laugh breaking out in a church.

There are no windows at the back of the house. It fits into a shelf that has been dug out of the hill, an extinct volcano, Carraig an Mhionnáin, the Rock of the Kid Goat. The house turns its back to the volcano and looks directly at the sea. In front are two big windows, floor to ceiling, one which opens as a patio door on to a stone terrace. A field then, full of long grass, July weeds and wild flowers – thistles, burdock, as well as eyebright, clover, buttercups, dandelions. Then, the Blasket Islands: the rounded hump of the Great Blasket directly in front, the elongated Inis Tuaisceart, the Dead Man, to the right, the north side. Not a single house or building impeded the view in 1976 – far down on the edge of the sea the sweet brown wooden house with blue gables, the MacEntee bungalow, built by Monsignor Padraig de Brún in the 1920s – the house where the Irish poet Máire Mhac an tSaoi spent her childhood holidays – sat. Already in 1976 the house had started its slow journey to decay and extinction but it always had a friendly, warm look, and it fitted into the landscape gently, almost naturally, just as Bo's house did.

Mandy and I gasped and made admiring comments about the view. Con put his hands on his hips knowingly, sighed deeply and agreed that it was a fine view all right. He'd seen it often before. Bo nodded and paid no attention to any of this. He had other concerns. Telling people where to sleep, where the bed linen was, showing them the bathroom.

He had already given some thought to who would sleep where: Mandy and I shared the big bedroom upstairs, Con had a bed in a smaller room, and Bo slept in the library, a study opening off the living room.

I took it for granted that all this organisation of rooms and food and space and time happened easily, naturally. Bo was the professor; he owned the house. I assumed he could just make the arrangements at the drop of a hat, without forethought. I had never taken responsibility for looking after guests and it never occurred to me that for anyone such an act of organisation would be challenging: where to put them, how to feed them.

It was harder in Dunquin than it would be in town. There was one small shop in the parish, within walking distance – the post office, where you could buy bread and milk and cigarettes and sweets and ice cream, every day, and sausages and rashers and cabbage and potatoes on Fridays. Kruger's, the pub, also stocked a few eclectic provisions: there you could get milk, or a can of beans, or a jar of strawberry jam. Otherwise you had to shop in Dingle and Bo didn't drive. So he had to plan the week strategically. He'd already bought what he hoped was enough food to see us through two days. On Wednesday, he would get the bus to Dingle and stock up again, with food that would last until Saturday, when all his guests would go home – after which, he would eat his dinner down the hill, in Molly's guest house. The planning of the week, which brought together people who did not know each other at all well, if at all, would have been difficult for anyone. For Bo, who was always nervous and anxious when it came to making practical arrangements – who was the sort of person who liked to be at the airport two or three hours before take-off, even in the old days when there was no such thing as security checks – it must have taken a huge amount of effort and caused at least some anxiety. But he did it, as he did everything which he considered to be his duty, without complaint and without showing signs of stress. 'I have been in the army,' was one of his sayings, referring to his year of military service, and meaning that nothing could really seem too challenging, after that horrible experience.

I soon guessed that I had been invited partly as a chaperone. Bo fancied Mandy. Any man would. She was beautiful in a soft, feminine, unintimidating way – she was a bit like Liv Ullmann, Liv in the country, with couldn't-be-bothered hair, jeans and a sloppy T-shirt. And apart from her physical attributes she had charm and wit. She teased Bo and argued with him, as if she were his equal. I treated him the way most of his Irish students did: meek and watchful. Mandy's peppery, bubbling spontaneity must have been a welcome relief from all the shy cunning and respectful scepticism that saturated the air of Belfield.

Not that there was anything doing. Mandy was living with someone else with whom she was desperately in love. They shared the kind of tiny cottage in Stoneybatter that had not yet become the last word in fashion for with-it young people – not quite yet. But it would very soon. Mandy and her man were the trendsetters. He owned the cottage; she had 'moved in' with him, and she talked about him all the time. She talked about him too much.

There had been more than one reason for Bo's neglect of his thesis duties.

He had suffered a minor nervous breakdown, precipitated by divorce from his wife and the fall-out from that, which he took very badly. He had been seeing a psychiatrist regularly and taking anti-depressants that made him tired and bloated.

The whole story was not told, to me, or to Mandy, that summer. We knew he was divorced, and in the process of buying a new apartment, because he talked about that quite a lot. The business of mortgages and insurance and so on subjected him to a lot of stress. It kept him in Dublin when he wanted to be in Kerry, collecting stories and writing. It filled his life with administrative problems, for which he had no taste or natural ability, although since he was meticulous and careful he handled them reasonably well: Bo was the sort of person who always answers a letter or pays a bill the day it arrives. But these chores distracted him; he had a tendency to be catastrophic and to feel overwhelmed by administrative challenges. (He could forget, sometimes, that he had been in the army.) The systems he was dealing with seemed unnecessarily inefficient, cumbersome and unpredictable – which they often were.

Con, and the car, left on Tuesday. Every morning, Bo spent an hour with Mandy, teaching her Irish. For the next few hours he transcribed tapes of stories collected from Mícheál Ó Gaoithín. After lunch, he sat with me at the kitchen table and discussed my thesis.

His method of working with students on a thesis was thorough and unusual. He read every word, with the student, and suggested changes and amendments as he went along. This laborious line editing demanded a great deal of his time – more than the majority of supervisors would ever be willing to give to students – but it was the method Bo had experienced himself, as a student of Dag Strömbäck in Uppsala, and he continued to use this intensive one-to-one method until his retirement. He was an outstanding editor, spotting every error, woolly thought, inaccurate observation – although occasionally due to the fact that he was working in what for him was a foreign language, small spelling errors could slip past his eagle eye. Not often, though, since his English was excellent, as was his Irish. Theories unsupported by evidence, pretension, or any kind of illogical thinking, never escaped him.

If Bo had a fault as a supervisor, it was that he could be too controlling. His intentions were the best, and his judgement almost invariably correct, but he could seem over-protective in his desire to prevent students from making wildly inaccurate assumptions and drawing false conclusions. Although he inspired almost all his students with his passionate interest in his subject, he did not encourage enough experimentation with methodology. His contempt for shoddy scholarship – that is, opinion that was not supported by evidence, theories that were generalisations and could not withstand scientific scrutiny – wrought in him occasional contempt for academics who employed shortcuts. Swedish folklorists of his own generation, who had dumped philology and the study of historical texts in favour of loosely defined sociological studies (of gardening, it could be, or weekend hobbies), he regarded with undisguised dismay. There were plenty of good reasons for his harsh judgement of the new wave of folklorists. He was a scholar of an old-fashioned kind – as a young man aged twenty-two, for instance, he had read the entire corpus of medieval Icelandic literature during one summer when he worked as a farm hand in Iceland. He had taken the time and trouble to learn several languages almost to perfection: his library contained substantial numbers of books in French, German, Spanish, Italian, Latin, Danish, Norwegian, as well as the medieval versions of most of those languages and the languages that he used more or less daily: Swedish, Irish, English and Icelandic. His knowledge of literature, folklore, and history was immense. Academic writing that was more akin to journalism than to scholarship as he knew it he had no time for. This meant that he was occasionally dismissive of new theories, and tended not to keep up with the times. For him, it didn't matter. In a sense he transcended the times. But for his students, it might sometimes have been important to be more in tune with the latest fashions in research. One result of this dismissal of many (although not all) of the latest theories was that some students, when they encountered them for the first time, usually during the year abroad, were utterly seduced by them and turned against Bo – he who had encouraged them to go abroad in the first place. They fell hook, line and sinker for the latest trends, took up a critical stance towards their old teacher, and, in his view, betrayed him and what he represented.

Back to the summer of 1976.

On Wednesday, Bo went to Dingle on the bus that stopped at the bottom of the hill to buy more groceries, and Oliver came from Dingle on a later bus to join the party in the house. He arrived as we were sitting around the table for the evening meal. The door was opposite the table, and he entered as on to a stage. Mandy's eyes widened when she saw him.

He was wearing blue jeans, as always, and a light beige raincoat, also as always. The suitcase he carried – rather oddly, for a young man visiting the country for a few days – was an expensive-looking one, made of a sort of tweed fabric that was sturdy enough, apparently, to withstand a blow from an icepick, should anyone want to try bashing it with one. He looked more like a basketball hero than a classical scholar. He was not what Mandy had expected, that was clear.

'I'll move out into the other room,' Mandy immediately offered.

I refused. 'It's fine. Stay on here.'

Bo was not sure how the room situation would work out. He knew Ireland was a strange place as far as sexual relations were concerned, very unlike Sweden, and kept his nose out of it. As it happened, Oliver and I had not had sex together, not properly, at this stage, although we had been a couple for over a year. It is a situation that is unthinkable nowadays, and Oliver, although admirably tolerant and understanding given that he was English, and came from quite a different and more liberated country, was beginning to find it all a bit ridiculous. But that was how it was. I had all the hang-ups of an Irish Catholic girl who has been rigorously conditioned to regard sex as the gateway to perdition. If you are told repeatedly that you will go to hell if you allow a man to penetrate you, and before that you will get pregnant and everyone will revile you and you will be in hell on earth, or at the bottom of the river, your attitude to the body is affected. Even though I was by now an atheist and regarded myself as sexually liberal, when it came to practice rather than theory I was very screwed up. Presumably most of the nation was in the same boat. It is a wonder that anyone in Ireland had sex at all. I think there is a great deal we don't know about sexual practices, within and outside of marriage, in Ireland in the twentieth century. Given the way most of us were brought up, I suspect that many of those young women who found themselves pregnant outside wedlock and cast into Magdalene laundries and the like were rape victims at one level or another. Or else totally ignorant of the facts of life.

I was happy to continue sharing a room with Mandy, while

Oliver was safely isolated in the small bedroom. I would kiss him and hug him, but I didn't want to have sex with him, especially not in someone else's house.

Over the next few days, the sun continued to shine, as it would all through the summer of 1976. The routine of Irish lessons and thesis editing continued exactly as before: depressed or not, Bo was a stickler for routine where writing and research were concerned. Oliver was writing his own thesis and so was perfectly happy to devote two thirds of the day to work. For the rest of the time, we walked in the rich dramatic landscape of Dunquin – to the beach at Clochar, where we picnicked and went for a swim in the rolling, crashing waves. On the way back, over the heathery hillside, Oliver, who loved all kinds of music, sang 'I Come from Alabama with a Banjo on My Knee'. In the evenings we went to Kruger's, a small shebeen-like establishment, with standing room only for the hordes of people who filled it on summer nights. Bo and Oliver loved it, the pints of Guinness, the dozens of real Dunquin men, one-time Blasket islanders, who leaned on the bar and spoke Irish. I didn't like pubs of any kind much and still less the kind of pub where you couldn't sit down, but I appreciated the special quality of this one – which was linguistic and cultural. One evening we visited Bab Feirtéir, Bo's favourite storyteller since Mícheál Ó Gaoithín had died in 1974. We asked her if she knew the story I was working on – 'With His Whole Heart'. But she didn't. She told other stories, however – 'The Mouse Who Was Late for Mass', and a few others. It was the first time I 'collected' folk tales: I hadn't been a folklore undergraduate so had not been on the annual field trips that were such a feature of that programme. It was thrilling to hear a storyteller narrating, especially by her own fireside.

Oliver loved everything: the pub, the Irish, the boats bobbing in and out on the choppy waves to the island. He was thrilled with the view of the Blaskets, and with the rich, dramatic landscape. He was thrilled with me: it was thanks to me after all that he was here in this iconic, historically fascinating, stunningly lovely place. Bo's invitation had given me status in his eyes. If the professor invites you to his summer house he must think your thesis is good was the reasoning. Bo didn't think it was good – he never thought anyone's thesis was good – but he believed it was a bit better than most, and that it could become good, if we worked on it hard enough.

Most attention in the house focused on Bo. He was the host and he was unlike anyone else we knew: learned, clever, handsome, Swedish. More friendly than most teachers, and also more reserved.

And more sad.

His heart, I could see it so easily, was broken. I knew the barest outline of the story. 'I am divorced from my wife.'

When you heard these facts about an adult, you just assumed everything was as straightforward as it sounded. Matter-of-fact decisions were made. We separated. These things happen.

It was the same as hearing that someone died, that someone had lost a wife or a husband to death. Blah. It's a line in a newspaper. You read it and a shadow falls on your cup of coffee. In a second the shadow vanishes, perhaps a nanoscar incises itself somewhere deep in your unconscious, but you have forgotten, you return to the business in hand, the cup of coffee, your busy immortal life.

These things happen. To other people. They'll get over it. They all seem to get over it, don't they? Heartache, love, joy and tears, the agony and the ecstasy, were the preserve of youth, I believed, or rather assumed, as my companions and I tumbled about in the whirling emotional oceans of our early twenties.

Older people like Bo swam in a different stream and had other things to occupy them, such as teaching and writing and being important. Divorced? So what? Could it really bother him much?

Only in his eyes I saw something that I recognised.

Heartbreak, behind the cheery laugh and quick wit and the enthusiastic energy. Behind the elegant face and the tweed coat of armour. I wasn't going to lift the visor; I wasn't going to ask questions. He would certainly have snubbed me, if I had begun to pry.

I caught a glimpse of him, behind the veil. And he knew I'd caught it. He knew I understood things that Oliver, for instance, would not. There was that understanding between us. We were members of the club of the X-ray eyes, the club of people who can see into the human heart.

I didn't delude myself that he saw anything in my eyes. He preferred Mandy's: sparkling, quick, and hurt in the way a child's eyes can be hurt. But he knew me, all right, because of what he read in my thesis, my essays. Even in the driest scholarship, emotional learning emerges, since stories and literature are about emotions, in folklore as in literature, in the Middle Ages as in the twenty-first century. As we analysed folk tales, and the poems of Chaucer, we realised we both knew how the human heart works. We could understand the depths of emotion that the poets and storytellers described in symbols and metaphors.

At the end of the week in Kerry, I believed I had something in common with Bo, apart from an interest in folklore. We were on the same emotional wavelength.

But of course it is easy to imagine such things, when you are falling in love.

BEFORE OUR DAY
'The forgotten fiancée'

That had been summer 1976. In 1977, Oliver and I became engaged, but by January 1978 our relationship was in stormy territory. I was still in love with him but the feeling was no longer reciprocated. I found it difficult to accept this. He was pulling away, sending the messages that are a sure indication that the carnival is over: he came late for dates, sometimes he didn't show up, he was impatient and distant when he did. Breaking up is hard to do, whichever side of the fence you are on. Oliver wanted to end the relationship, but didn't want to be cruel. Unfortunately this was an impossible goal.

I was in denial. But the situation was uncomfortable, to put it mildly. I made an excuse – the only person who demanded this excuse was myself – to escape. The last week in January, I decided to go to Donegal. A strange place to head off to at that time of year.

I was scheduled to give a paper to the postgraduate seminar group in the Folklore Department in February, and decided that I would write this paper in a B&B in Gortahork. I had the impression that folklorists did things like this: travelled to remote Gaeltacht regions in the west of Ireland to do fieldwork, research. To write.

Bo was very enthusiastic. I was closer to him now than before, more relaxed, and, as a doctoral student, had a little more status in college than I had enjoyed previously. He advised me to drop into Seán Ó hEochaidh, a retired full-time collector, who spent his life collecting folklore in Donegal for the Irish Folklore Commission. He lived in the post office in Gortahork, just across the street from McFadden's Hotel.

'Ask him if he has heard a version of "With His Whole Heart",' Bo advised. 'You never know.'

Oliver did not approve of the trip.

'Why don't you write it at home? Or in the library?'

He didn't enjoy having me around, but neither did he want me to go away.

I had no good answer to his question. People like to remove themselves from their usual environment to write things: to cottages in the country, to institutions in other countries, even to hotels. But why such places should be more encouraging or inspiring than a quiet room at home, or a table in a library, I don't actually know.

Still, how nice that he didn't want me to go away, even for a week! Just as he had not wanted me to go away for a year, to Algeria. I interpreted it as a sign that he still half-loved me, in spite of all the indications to the contrary.

I got off the bus at the road which leads to Cnoc na Naomh, and carried my bag and typewriter down towards the sea, to the McFadden's bungalow – lots of McFaddens, around here. A thin sheet of snow covered the ground like sugar. The crisp air was spiked with the smell of turf smoke, like some delicious herb in a glass of champagne. Stars crowded the sky. A nice yellow moon, almost full. What with all the moonlight and starlight and snowlight, it was not dark at all, and my heart was light too, as I made my way along the road. What an intrepid thing to do! How brave, how unusual I am!

Breedeen, the woman of the house, thought so too.

She was a round motherly woman, with a round rosy face and a round cap of black curly hair, and she greeted me and showed me to my room with great warmth and politeness but an undertone of amusement. It was obvious that whatever she had been expecting, it wasn't this slight girl of twenty-three, carrying a typewriter and a rucksack.

McFadden's was a long low bungalow, with white walls, picture windows, and a green tiled roof – the type of bungalow that had been springing up all over the west of Ireland from the 1960s, during the decades of modernisation, which were also decades of destruction. They were modelled on designs in a best-selling paperback called *Bungalow Bliss*, already coming under attack from the young journalists in Dublin, who would soon inspire a backlash against this latest kind of vernacular architecture. It had a big front garden, and on one side a shop, on the other the ruins of the old country cottage that had been the original dwelling house and was now used to store junk. Its thatched roof had caved in, and there was a bit of galvanised iron on one end, forming a partial shelter.

I was given a big bedroom, painted primrose yellow, with fresh flowery curtains on the window and a yellow wash-hand basin in the corner. The radiator was lukewarm, the default temperature for central heating systems in Ireland then, when it existed at all, being about fifteen degrees. An electric heater, the little fat kind with two bars, was in the corner, not switched on, but Breedeen told me to use it to boost the temperature should I need it. Then she showed me a sitting room, where I could sit and read or write by the turf fire, and the dining room – a big conservatory at the back of the house, furnished with eight tables, and obviously designed to cater for a houseful of summer visitors. That's where I would eat my breakfast and evening meal for the duration of my stay.

I was the only guest at the moment, f course. Who comes to the Gaeltacht in January?

The week passed, and I was happy. I walked to Gortahork, about two or three miles away, and called in on Seán Ó hEochaidh. A plump pleasant-faced man whose looks reminded me of my father's: medium height, square body and square head. Thick white hair, twinkling eyes. No, he didn't know my story, but he advised me to visit a storyteller, Joe Mac Eachmharcaigh, who lived near to my B&B, in the townland of Doire Chonaire.

I set out to find Joe on the second night, also crisp and moonlit. I tramped along a bog road, serenaded by barking dogs, intoxicated by the turf smoke. It began to snow. Overjoyed, I thought I was like the Brothers Grimm, going out to collect stories in the countryside around Kassel at the beginning of the nineteenth century – obviously I knew very little about the Brothers Grimm, or I wouldn't have drawn any comparisons. I imagined them as middle-aged men, did not know that they were about my age when they began to collect tales, did not know that they seldom if ever went out tramping around the countryside, in winter or summer, but relied on their friends, often women, to send them the stories in letters. But it was a magical association, which quickened my step and helped me overcome my fear of the crazy dogs, and my shyness at barging in on a complete stranger.

I would tell Bo about this, and I knew he would be pleased, and proud of his good student, following in his own footsteps. For he, as a young student, had tramped the countryside in Kerry, and in Iceland, seeking out storytellers and collecting their tales. I felt, under the starry night, that I was part of a chain of tradition that certainly went back to the age of romanticism, to 1812, the year of the publication of the Grimms' collection of fairy tales, the groundbreaking book that was the catalyst for folktale collecting and comparative folklore studies all over Europe. I was simultaneously a participant in that great project that had been going on for almost two hundred years: the folklore project, the tradition project. I was becoming one of the conservationists who both discover and save the culture of the world. That's what I felt, crunching through the snow, under the stars.

Like the B&B, Joe Mac Eachmharcaigh's house was cheek by jowl with a derelict whitewashed cottage, grass and weeds abundant on its collapsing thatched roof; the beautiful ruined old cottage was side by side with a modern home. But Joe didn't live in a big bungalow. His home was a little prefab hut, what was known in Donegal as a chalet. Turf smoke puffed out of a steel pipe that served as a chimney. No dog, until I knocked on the door. Then a ferocious barking and a man's voice saying *Druid do bhéal, druid do bhéal!* Or something like that.

Joe was shocked to see me on the doorstep, a stranger in the snow.

'*Tar isteach a thaisce!*'

He welcomed me into his room.

It was like stepping into an oven, wonderfully hot after the freezing temperature outdoors. And the room was cosy. Outside, the house looked like a temporary office on a building site. But this grim exterior led to a traditional Donegal kitchen. A range in the middle of the gable wall, a table under the window. Down at the back wall, a red settle bed. Just like the old cottage I had often stayed in as a child.

The room embraced me with its warmth. I felt perfectly at home. It was like opening a shabby old book and entering a fairy tale. My excitement surged.

Joe was old. Maybe sixty, maybe seventy, maybe eighty. I couldn't tell. Old is old. He was tall, with a wrinkled face the colour of turf dust, strong nose, wide mouth. Dressed any old way, an old jumper, some sort of ancient trousers, too big for him.

The first thing he did was introduce me to his aunt, who lay, all day and night, in the bed at the back of the house. A tiny white-haired woman, she was playing with her rosary beads. She was delighted to meet me, and welcomed me a thousand times.

'Would you like a fag?' Joe asked.

'I would,' she said.

He propped her up a bit on a pillow, lit a Woodbine and put it in her hand. She smoked happily, half lying against the pillow.

'Would you like one?' Abruptly he turned to me, as if he had just remembered that I was there. He had a slight stutter that disappeared once he spoke at any length.

I declined but accepted the offer of a cup of tea. The cup looked as if it hadn't been washed, but I drank the tea anyway. Asked my question about the story. No, he hadn't heard it. But if I wanted to come back tomorrow he would tell other stories. He knew lots of stories. He knew dozens. I should come at night – like now – because he'd be busy during the day.

He spoke a mixture of Irish and English. I spoke only Irish to him, and he understood my Dublin Irish, but was afraid that I would not understand his strong Donegal dialect. So he said things like, '*an bealach mór, nó an bóthar, nó* the road.' To make sure I would get it.

Next day I hitchhiked to Falcarragh, a village that is a bit bigger than Gortahork. In a small hardware shop there I found a cassette recorder, and purchased it for what was quite a princely sum: £50. But I earned a good salary, I could afford things. I was not going to miss the opportunity to record Joe now that I was walking in the footsteps of the Brothers Grimm. I also bought a bottle of whiskey. Bo did this when he was visiting his storytellers, sometimes, if they were the type who liked a drink. He would buy one of the little bottles – a quarter, a naggin? But I didn't want to take any chances so I splashed out on a full-size one.

Joe told three or four stories, over the week, and sang many songs. The stories are long *Märchen*, or fairy tales – 'The Boy Who Wanted to Know What Fear Is', 'The Brave Tailor', and 'The Maiden of Light'.

He sat at the side of the table facing the window, and I sat in the corner under the cupboard where he kept his tea and sugar and other groceries. The cassette recorder, a silver box about the size of a box of Uncle Ben's rice, sat on the blue and red oilcloth. I used the batteries, because I was reluctant to use his electricity. It was a simple machine to operate – you slipped the empty cassette cartridge into its slot, and closed it. There was a row of keys or buttons at one end of the recorder. One with a warning red dot was the Record key. There were two for Fast Forward and Rewind, and another two for Play and Stop. Joe waited expectantly while I fiddled with the machine. He held the little microphone himself.

I pressed the Record button: you had to press hard to get it going.

'*Bhfuil sé ag obair?* Is it going?'

'*Tá.* One, two, three.'

I tested it. Stopped it. Rewound. Pressed Play.

Joe's voice, a little anxious, played back. He smiled. My 'one, two, three' was on the cassette too, sounding muffled and childish.

'*Tá sé ag obair!*'

'Okay. We'll start now!'

I pressed the Record button again.

'*Bhfuil scéal ar bith agat?*'

'*Táim chun scéal a inseacht duit anois agus sé an scéal atá mé chun inseacht duit ná Maighdean an tSolais …*'

He inclined his head on one side, and began to tell the story. His voice rises and falls. He looks at me as he begins but as the tale goes on he looks at the window, he gets drawn into his own story, carried away by it, although now and then he withdraws from it and makes a comment on a character or an action.

'*Bhí sí maith dó, nach raibh?*' He looks at me as he describes an episode in which a girl carries out impossible tasks for the hero, and then spreads out a tablecloth on the ground and gives him all the food and drink he could desire.

I was transported by joy. The story was one of the great international fairy tales, unknown in the storybook tradition or Disneyworld, but one of those that was outstandingly popular in Irish oral tradition in the past. I did not know it very well and was interested in hearing it told. But what was more enthralling was the sense I had of listening to something that had been handed down from mouth to mouth for many generations. There was, in the little hot kitchen, a sense of connection to a chain of storytellers going back through the centuries, back to the Middle Ages – earlier, because some of the episodes in this particular story were documented in Greek literature, six hundred years BC. Books link you to the past too, of course. But the line of oral transmission is more moving, because it's so fragile. A book can survive unread for centuries in a library, and then be rediscovered. A story that is not written down depends entirely on being told again and again for its survival. If people stop telling it, it vanishes off the face of the earth. The chain of oral transmission is indescribably delicate. Unlike booklore, oral lore is intangible. And in 1978 it was very rare to find anywhere in Europe a storyteller who knew tales he or she had learnt from earlier narrators. The *Märchen* are sometimes called wonder tales, or tales of magic, in English. The stories are indeed wondrous because of their fantastic content; in them the human imagination is in full and glorious flight. But even more wondrous is the experience of listening to a tale told by a good storyteller, a tale that has survived by being told again and again by many individual anonymous people over hundreds of years, and is brought to life once again in a prefabricated hut in Donegal.

I couldn't articulate my feelings with any precision, as I listened to Joe, as I recorded his voice and his stories and songs. Gratitude, astonishment? Pleasure, joy? There was no word for this: for the sense of being awestruck, of hearing the voices, many voices, of the past, transmitted over centuries. It was like listening to the dead, although the story was as alive as the dogs barking in the winter farmyards, or the waves crashing against Bloody Foreland. It was like meeting the poets of the thirteenth century, and every century since then. It was like touching an invisible glinting chain that goes back through the ages, and getting an electric shock from it: small, thrilling, like the shock from some sea creature in the depths of the ocean.

It was an experience like no other, an experience I felt very lucky to have, because who has it? Just a handful of the chosen, the self-selected, the ones who are drawn to this sort of thing, for reasons that they don't usually analyse themselves. Why had I chosen to study folklore? I could come up with reasons – I was not far removed from the traditional communities of Ireland, and as soon as I found myself in the Folklore Department I felt a powerful draw to the material; I also loved the scientific methodology, the empirical investigation of documents and recordings, the precision of the way folklore was studied. But in the end I don't know why some of us are attracted by this kind of exploration, while others are not. Just as I don't know why some people become writers and others don't (and both instincts, the instinct to study folk literature and the instinct to be a writer, are linked; I'm sure of that). One can speculate, and come up with more than one reason. But in the end there's a mystery about it.

What is certain is that the voice of this old man in the hut perched on a bog in Donegal carried me away, to the most distant places, to the crepuscular landscapes, the fire-lit caves, where the work and the play of the human imagination first began.

It was a cold wet Friday night when I got back home to Ranelagh. Oliver called around almost immediately. He didn't come into the dining room, where my parents were sitting by the fire watching TV, or to the kitchen, where I had been reading. He stood in the hall, the door open behind him.

He wanted to break it off.

He insisted on explaining why.

And, oh, there were several reasons, ranging from my unsuitability to be a wife (I was feminist and independent; I went off to Donegal on my own without discussing it with him first) to his lack of attraction for me. He wanted to tell me all the reasons, all about it.

I knew I should feel sad, traumatised, overwhelmed by grief.

All I wanted was to get some sleep. Go, go away and let me sleep, I thought. But he stood with one foot in the door, talking, going on and on and on like a salesman persuading me to buy something. To buy the break-up, the reasons for it, the logic of it all.

Go away. Please, just go away.

After a traumatic relationship break-up – as after a death – you feel nothing for a while, except a desire to get away from the scene of the crime. I felt like that in the hour after Bo died. All I wanted was to get away from the hospital, to run from the deathbed. At these dreadful moments you shut down. Your mind and body are in a state of shock, and you're temporarily numb to deep emotion. Those most affected by a tragedy don't scream or cry, like people in movies. They are paralysed. It is exactly the same as a scald or a burn to the flesh. Have you noticed what happens? For minutes after the boiling water scalds your skin you feel absolutely nothing. Later the pain comes. The self-help books, the psychiatrist's studies of grief, say that this is the body's way of protecting you from unendurable pain. By the time it hits you, your body has grown that bit stronger.

Next morning, when I woke up, I knew something was wrong. But for a minute I couldn't remember what.

Oh yes.

I was no longer engaged to Oliver. That was it.

Unbelievable. Yesterday, he was my fiancé. Today, he was not. I wouldn't be seeing him for lunch, or after work, or tomorrow either, or the next day.

He was out of my story now, he who had been the main actor for three years. Only eight or nine hours ago he had been on the doorstep and now he wouldn't be on the doorstep again. Ever? How could that be true?

The next day I applied for the scholarship to go to Denmark. I also bought an evening newspaper, and looked at the small ads for flats and bedsitters. Even if I wasn't getting married I could move out of my parents' house, at long last. I could have a bedsitter of my own.

DAY 2

'Let me not to the marriage of true minds admit impediment'

What I wore: a salmon-coloured frock, with a small terracotta print. A lace trim on the collar. Empire line. A rust-coloured tweed jacket.

I wore clothes like that, although I was twenty-four – ancient, as it seemed to me then. Modest loose clothes, covering the knees, even though I was slim and had good enough legs and would have looked fine in a miniskirt. Minis were over anyway, of course. It was 1978. Laura Ashley was the designer of choice. This dress had been bought somewhere else, in a sale, because soon I would not have a good salary or any salary. I'd be back to the bargain basement, on student rations.

But I often bought a new dress.

My hair was long, black, shining. It was tucked behind my ears and flowing down my back to the halfway mark between my shoulders and waist. I never let it get as far as my waist. I could have had a yard of hair. But something stopped me. It would have been too much. There were unspoken rules, in the air around you, that you understood although they were never articulated. Don't go too far. Even where hair is concerned.

I was to meet him at his apartment. Then we were going out to dinner. My bedsitter was close to town, in Rathmines, and Bo lived in Booterstown. That seemed far away, far out. Blackrock. A place you went to very occasionally, to swim in the open-air baths, which I never had liked. Too cold, too crowded. Too ugly and uncomfortable. Most people I knew lived in Ranelagh and Rathmines, either because that's where they came from, or because they were renting a bedsitter. Ranelagh was still full of bedsitters. Some people thought it was all bedsitters but there were always plenty of families, scattered around, on the shabby roads, like the one my parents lived on, and on the posh roads, in Beechwood. It was a 'mixed area', back then, quite unlike the fashionable expensive urban village it has since become.

I got a bus from town, from Merrion Square, the 7 or the 8, one of the buses that went along the coast out to Dún Laoghaire or Dalkey. A lovely summer's evening. The bus crept out through Ballsbridge, past Merrion Gates, the Tara Towers, Booterstown Marsh. A twenty-minute journey but not one I was in the habit of taking, so it felt very long. I kept looking out, afraid I would miss my stop. But no. At the Punchbowl I got off. Traffic roared along the Rock Road. I crossed at the traffic lights where that road met Booterstown Avenue.

There are old houses at that end of the avenue, three-storey, Victorian or Edwardian, the same as the houses in Rathmines. Rather gloomy-looking. And the avenue is dark and shadowy at that point, even on a summer's evening. I walked up, about a hundred yards.

Then I stopped in my tracks like a horse who senses an evil presence.

Like a rabbit caught in the headlights.

I couldn't do it.

I couldn't go and have dinner with Bo. He was twenty years my senior. He was my professor.

He was really *old*.

I had stopped outside the grey stone wall of one of those old houses. My stomach churned, and everything else. Terror is what I was feeling. Deep visceral fear.

*

After the meeting in Belfield, about a week ago, I had walked on air.

I was in love, in love with Bo.

I had been in love with him for a long time, in a way, ever since I had read in his eyes that his heart was broken.

And there were other reasons. His good looks. His Swedishness. His enthusiasm, brilliance, learning. His fearlessness and confidence and wit.

'We are all in love with him,' someone had said to me, a year earlier, at a party.

And now I was in love with him and he was in love with me.

For the past week, since we met in Belfield and since his phone call, I had gone around nursing my delicious secret. My new, strange, exotic love.

But now, as it was coming to the point, to the fateful moment, the cream turned sour. My stomach churned. My feet would not take another step. My body was screaming: Stop.

It was that, rather than thoughts as such. The reality biting, physically. The romantic dream stopping and reality reasserting itself.

Or was it just society imposing its norms? Asserting its taboos. Not for the first time. Thou shalt not:

Have sex before marriage.

Get pregnant before marriage.

Fall in love with an older man.

Marry an older man.

On a May evening at the bottom of Booterstown Avenue, under a tall, gloomy Victorian house which blocked out the sun.

Fear paralyses.

What would people say? What would they say tonight, as Bo and I ate dinner somewhere? I was young enough to be his daughter. That's what they would say. That's what they would think. I'd look ridiculous, in my salmon-pink, granny-print frock, with my long black hair, on a date with Bo, that old man of forty-three. They would laugh, they'd disapprove, they'd say, how absurd! How pitiful! Can't she get someone her own age? She's pathetic.

So many taboos, in 1978.

I turned around and walked slowly away, dragging my legs back towards the bus stop.

In front of me, the railway station, the sea wall, the sea.

The blue bay of Dublin. Howth Head across the water.

Sea looks cold and cruel, when you are sad or anxious. Even blue sea. And even on the best of days the Irish Sea can look cold and cruel. In that sea there is a bleakness, always.

The sea hurt me. Hurt me in my gut. The oceans of the world tumbled around my heart. Yes, the line in 'Eveline' reflects truth. You can feel like that. Like Eveline, I was paralysed by fear of the unknown. Like Eveline, I would go home to the hopelessness that was familiar, rather than the hope that was unknown.

To my bedsitter?

To my parents' house?

I hated it there.

They were kind and tolerant parents. Much better than most. And the house was comfortable enough. I shared a bedroom with my sister but I had my own little room to write and study in. The sitting room all to myself most of the time, if I wanted to read or listen to music, since my parents were always at the fire with the television in the dining room. The house was old and pretty, although neither I nor anyone else appreciated that back then. Badly furnished in what I thought was bad taste – 1960s taste. Ugly.

I hated it.

How could I tell my parents I was dating a forty-three-year-old man? Foreign. Protestant. Divorced. With a daughter who was almost as old as me – I tended to forget about her because she was living abroad.

It was the forty-three-year-old aspect that would bother them most, I guessed, correctly. Oliver was Protestant and foreign and that hadn't mattered. Of course, English didn't count as foreign.

They hardly seemed aware of his religion, There was much more fuss about these differences in fiction than in life, as far as I could see. Or perhaps my parents were just more tolerant than most, more flexible, more loving?

Age was another thing.

These reservations, fears, had been slipping in and out of my mind over the past week, at exactly the same time as my heart had been singing with joy. In love, in love, I am in love! My sense of being in love had lightened my heart and my feet and had put my step and my bloodstream in rhythm with the birds singing their hearts out in the gardens, with the sun sparkling down on the slates of the little Dublin houses. But under all that joyous music a dark and heavy chord, like a slow heavy instrument, a cello, the bass violin, played quietly and morosely away, while the harpsichord of being in love danced and pranced loudly on top. The voice of reason and caution.

Too different. Nobody will stand for it. It will be much worse than hair to your waist, hair to your ankles. They'll laugh at you, and pass remarks behind your back, and sneer. There was a lot of prejudice about age differences, then. It was always assumed that a young woman married an older man for one thing only: his money, or – since according to the stereotype these matches were mainly made in rural Ireland, or in plays by John B. Keane – his farm.

Bo didn't have a farm, or any money, but I could see the faces of those who would sneer. Girls I had been in primary school with. Whose mothers gossiped with my mother. Who had known me when I made my First Communion, got my first period, got the scholarship to secondary school. They were people who looked out for me, and also people who had standards, who kept me on the straight and narrow track.

The voice of the censor. Under the surface, checking and balancing. These people had said, when I was studying too much, why not get out and enjoy life? They said, when I started my PhD, sometimes men don't like girls to be too educated.

They said things that would one day seem outrageous, but some of which made sense. They were wise, in their way. They wanted what was best for me. And the best thing, the easiest thing, is the simplest: conform. Be like everyone else. Fit in.

There was much more pressure to fit in in 1978 than there is now, I think. And there were only a few ways to do it. Our society was not pluralistic or tolerant, but narrow, restrictive, punitive. Homosexuality was illegal. Divorce was illegal. Abortion, of course, was illegal. Even contraception was illegal. It's almost impossible for a young person growing up in today's Ireland to imagine how many restrictions there were on every aspect of sexual life. The legal restrictions were fundamentalist. And, apart from the law of the land, there were many more taboos, imposed by the Catholic church, and by society itself.

All the thoughts jumbled now, became a physical force that was driving me back to the bus stop, away from Bo.

I didn't even have to cross the road, to get the bus back to town. It stopped here, a bit up from the corner, where there was a shop that sold bicycles. The traffic flowed towards me, from the south on the way north, towards Ranelagh and Rathmines and town. It felt cold, on the Rock Road, with the fumes and noise of the cars, the bleak bay to the left, the bicycle shop to the right.

Then I saw Bo.

In my mind's eye.

Waiting in his flat.

In his tweed jacket, smoking his pipe, reading, looking up, glancing at his watch, wondering where I was, what was delaying me.

He was not a stranger, but a teacher, a friend I had known for years. He wasn't a person you couldn't trust. The complete opposite.

I saw his happy eyes, his laughing smile.

The poem he had sent me last week. A love poem written by him, the only love poem I ever received in my life. The other poem he had recited to me when we walked across the field in Belfield, and had given me a book – the poems of Charles D'Orléans. But as he handed it to me he recited one by Yeats.

When you are old and grey and full of sleep,
And nodding by the fire, take down this book,
And slowly read, and dream of the soft look
Your eyes had once, and of their shadows deep;

How many loved your moments of glad grace,
And loved your beauty with love false or true,
But one man loved the pilgrim soul in you,
And loved the sorrows of your changing face.

(Could there be a more powerful chat-up line?)
I could not disappoint him.
At the corner by the bicycle shop I stood for ten minutes. The bus came, the 7, but I didn't put out my hand. I watched it sailing down the Rock Road towards the city.
And I turned around again.
Up the avenue I walked. Past the old houses, and the church and the newer houses. First I went slowly, then speeded up until my feet were flying along the footpath. Past the big pub on the bend in the road the sun was stronger. By the time I reached the apartments, set back a little from the road in a plain green park with a row of saplings by the outer wall, the sun was strong, and the new buildings, glass and white concrete, were bathed in warm yellow light.
His was number three.
There were hardly any apartment complexes in Dublin then. This was one of the first on the south side, and it had been built so that the apartments looked like little houses, two storeys high. Each flat had its own front door. Bo's was on the ground floor.
An ordinary door with glass panels, and a box bay window beside it.
I pressed the small black bell.
He opened the door immediately.

'Here you are, here you are!'

He opened his arms, embraced me, kissed me.

There was no reservation in his hug. He smothered me with kisses. He poured endearments over me. My darling, my dearest little darling.

His skin was warm and leathery, and his tweed coat was rough against my cotton frock. He smelt of pipe smoke and his mouth was large, soft, firm.

He felt enormous, although I was tall myself, not little at all. But I felt small and cherished, enfolded in those tweed arms, in that warm homespun embrace. He pulled me into his aura, as a bear hugs a cub. He transmitted his energy, his enthusiasm, his optimism, so that I was reinvigorated.

This was the only possible place to be.

We walked down the avenue, hand in hand – our relationship was to be kept a secret until I had finished my PhD, but the secretiveness had not started yet, on this first night, and indeed someone spotted us! We walked along the seafront to the restaurant where Bo had reserved a table. It was by the harbour in Dún Laoghaire. A big grey stone building without windows, forbidding on the outside, like a fortress. Inside, a luxurious cave. Soft candlelight, white tablecloths, silver and crystal. Too formal, but I didn't know much about restaurants. Perhaps this was where he always liked to eat?

'I did not tell you! It is my birthday.'

I was taken aback.

'Happy birthday!'

'Don't you want to know what age I am?'

'Yes.'

'I don't suppose you feel like singing "Happy Birthday"?'

He looked around. There was a general sense of hush in the restaurant. A few couples, who looked old, really old, were eating quietly. The women glanced at me, glanced away again, minding their own business. A waiter in black glided around importantly.

There were no prices on my menu.

'I know what I'm going to have!' he declared. 'Prawns provençale.'

'I'll have that too.'

I didn't want to order something that cost more than what he was having.

So we talked about Provence. The troubadours. The love poem he had written for me was a rondeau, based on a kind of rhythm used by Charles D'Orléans, who was not, of course, a troubadour as such. But Bo liked the idea of Provence. He had gone there for a holiday during the Christmas break, alone, the year after his divorce.

'What was it like?'

He reflected.

'Absolutely horrible,' he said.

I laughed.

'It would probably be better with a friend.'

'Much, much better, my dear darling!'

A thing I did not know then – anyone would know it now – was that provençale, attached to food, means tomato sauce. Prawns in tomato sauce with rice. They were okay, but I hoped not terribly expensive, since they weren't all that special and there weren't very many of them. Six or seven prawns in tomato sauce. Like so many things, prawns were more exotic then than they are now.

We got a taxi home and I spent the night with him, on the blue sofa that could be made into a double bed. Making love with him was easy, as easy as going for a walk – mainly because, not being Irish, he just took it for granted that it would happen.

DAY 11,991

Halloween

I listened to the news on Radio 1 as I tidied up the cottage. There had been a fatal collision on the road between Monaghan and Castleblayney. I clocked it with the second of dismay one feels on hearing this commonplace news, wondered who had been killed. Some young man no doubt, speeding on that stretch of road, where we would drive later. Death is an everyday occurrence, obviously, visiting families as often as birth or marriage. But it was not knocking on my door that day so I ignored it, as we must do to get on with life.

We locked up at about ten, and set off, stopping on the boreen to deposit the plastic sacks of rubbish with a neighbour, Charlie, as we had pre-arranged. I had cleaned out the freezer, which had been full of food years past its sell-by date, and so there were a few black sacks. Bonnie, Charlie's dog, was not outside, which was just as well, because the sack would have driven any dog crazy. It stank to high heaven: overnight the frozen contents had melted, and were clearly rotten. The pong lingered in the car and on my hands for some hours, and I worried that I had left it to Charlie to dispose of the disgusting stuff. I was still in the zone where one worries about small offences, or possible offences. The zone of the normal.

On the way back, we stopped at a restaurant attached to a garden centre on the outskirts of Monaghan town and had lunch. Bo ordered a prawn sandwich once again, to my amusement: he was being reckless with shellfish, probably because he was still feeling a sense of relief thanks to his recent clean bill of health. We lingered in the garden centre, which was, to our surprise, already stocked with Christmas decorations and paraphernalia. I bought a small white tree that took my fancy. It was beautiful, and looked like a birch tree covered in frost. I knew exactly where I would put it, when we decorated the house for Christmas, although it seemed premature to be thinking of such matters before Halloween had even passed. 'No harm in being prepared!' said Bo, comfortingly.

Normal time.

Not far outside Monaghan the motorway between Castleblayney and Carrickmacross was closed, cordoned off, gardaí directed us to a side road. I remembered the fatal accident I had heard reported on the radio that morning. So they were still examining the scene. I sighed. What did I feel? Frustration, mainly. What a waste – fatal accidents happened frequently on that stretch of road. I couldn't imagine anything else, who he was, how his family felt. Needless death, and an inconvenience for us. We took the detour, which brought us along a narrow country road for several miles.

We got back to Dublin at about seven o'clock in the evening. The house was dark and cold.

Bo complained of a sore toe.

When we were going to bed, I had a look at it. The third toe on his right foot had a white blister on the tip, with a black centre. The toe was swollen.

'I think you should go to the doctor tomorrow,' I said. 'That foot specialist you saw two or three years ago told us we shouldn't hang about if anything went wrong with your feet.'

Bo had been worried about his feet for a long time. He often got severe cramps in his calf, and the circulation to his feet was very poor. The blue veins that criss-crossed his uppers like maps disturbed him, and he was often convinced that there was a problem. The podiatrist, in the Blackrock Clinic, had assured us that there was no real problem, apart from poor circulation, and told us not to worry. 'But if you cut your foot or anything like that, go to a doctor straight away – don't waste time.'

I googled 'feet' – perhaps I googled 'gangrene'? – and saw images of toes that looked a bit like Bo's. I wondered if he had dry gangrene. Creeping gangrene? I determined to go to the doctor first thing in the morning.

This was my first mistake, a wrong diagnosis based on googling.

I had a busy schedule on Thursday. At 6.30 p.m., I was due to launch a children's book, *The Secret of the Sleeveen*, by Brenda Ennis, in the Irish Writers' Centre, and later, at 9.30 p.m., I was performing at a big 'concert', an event in honour of the National Folklore Collection, and a fundraiser, which was taking place in Liberty Hall. I was doing a short presentation on the Urban Folklore Project. Although I had written my book launch speech and my presentation for the concert in Donegal, I still had some phone calls to make, to ensure that the clips of sound recordings I wanted to play at the concert had been collected from the Folklore Archive, and that all was well. I had left a DVD with the recordings for collection in the archive on Friday, before we went to Donegal. But somehow I anticipated a glitch. And a glitch occurred – nobody had collected the DVD and at this stage nobody knew where it was.

We went to the medical centre. The doctor we usually saw was not available so we saw another GP. On visits to consultants, of which there had been many, I usually went in to the meeting with Bo. But on this occasion I stayed in the waiting room. Why?

I know exactly why.

Three weeks earlier, we had been in Bruff in Limerick, where Bo was giving a lecture in memory of his colleague and good friend, Dáithí O hÓgáin, who died of cancer in 2011. Bo gave his talk on Friday night. On Saturday, there was a packed schedule of lectures and presentations, followed by an outing to Lough Gur in the afternoon. Bo went to all the lectures. I took a break from the final session of the morning, and met him and others for lunch in a pub before the Lough Gur outing. Everything ran late at this event so by the time Bo got to the pub we had about fifteen minutes to spare for lunch, before the bus was due to depart for the trip. He had to go to the loo. While he was gone, a waitress took the order, and I ordered my own sandwich and exactly the same for Bo – since I knew he wouldn't be fussy and, of course, know what he likes to eat. I noticed, or thought I noticed, one of his colleagues giving me a sharp look, suggesting that I was being disrespectful, patronising, not considering that Bo might like to place his own order. It occurred to me that yes, I could be too bossy.

That's what influenced me that day in the waiting room. I was still feeling guilty about that sandwich. I thought it would be good for Bo to be alone with the doctor, that he didn't need me around all the time.

Bo came out of the doctor's office in cheerful mood. The toe problem was just gout, not anything serious. Bo has had gout for about twenty years – he first got it when we were on a camping holiday in Italy in 1993. It recurred periodically, and was treated with Difene, an anti-inflammatory, which usually cured it very quickly. The gout always affected Bo's big toe, however, not any of the others, and that is why we didn't recognise it this time. I wondered about the white blister on Bo's toe but thought it might be the result of a cut, by the neighbouring nail.

Gout. Not gangrene then. What a relief!

'He prescribed a new kind of medicine,' Bo said, by which he meant one he himself had not used before. 'It's very strong and can have side effects but I'll try it.'

We collected the pills in the local pharmacy and drove home.

I had to phone the young woman who was organising the evening's concert to discuss the fate of my sound recordings. I also needed to buy sweets and nuts for the children who would call to the house that night, because it was Halloween. And I had an appointment with the hairdressers.

Too many things to do on one day.

Bo's toe was still sore. So he went back to bed. I was cross with him, and told him he shouldn't have eaten all that shellfish – which had almost certainly caused this gout. I felt pressurised, and wondered how I would deal with the schedule for the night – the thought of pulling out of either of the two commitments was unthinkable – which shows how silly we human beings are. The book could easily have been launched without me – there were if anything too many speakers. The concert in Liberty Hall had a packed programme and was also far too long – in fact, by the time I appeared on the stage, at 10.30 p.m. that night, some people in the audience had already left to catch their buses home.

Bo asked, how many of these pills should I take?

I didn't have my glasses – where were they? Not there. I snapped at him, told him to read the label himself. I got irritated when Bo forgot that I couldn't read without glasses – it had been several years since I could do that.

Rather impatiently, he had a look at it. Three once a day, he said.

I was surprised and said, that's unusual, isn't it?

I was standing at my dressing table, maybe brushing my hair, and Bo was in bed. The room was rather dark, although it was now about noon. He popped three pills into his mouth impatiently and swallowed them, without water. I was alarmed. I ran downstairs, found my glasses, came back up and read the label.

'It says one three times a day!' I said. 'How could you have been so bloody stupid?'

I ran downstairs again. Why? There is a phone by our bed. I suppose I ran down to get the telephone directory, which is in the hall beside the main phone. In the bright big kitchen, I phoned the surgery and explained to the receptionist what had happened. She put me through to the doctor. Thank goodness he is still there, I was thinking. I was still in ordinary time, where doctors leave the surgery at some particular time on the clock, where the time on the clock matters. He said he would phone the hospital, and ring back. He rang back quite quickly.

'It's not a toxic dose,' he said. 'If it is a toxic dose, you could take him to the hospital and get an antidote. But it will probably be all right. If he gets sick, take him to the hospital.'

But what does 'if he gets sick' really mean? Did I really take this in? No. Why didn't I ask him, 'What do you mean, sick?' Why didn't I say, 'Well, let's play safe?' I know why. I was busy. I had stuff to do, commitments, I wasn't about to let people down – the writer of the children's book, the organisers of the concert. I didn't want to go to the hospital and I was relieved this wasn't necessary.

I read the leaflet that came with the pills. (For some reason, the name of the pills reminded me of Chaucer, and 'The Pardoner's Tale', one of Bo's favourites, came to mind. It is a story about poison, and the impossibility of cheating fate, or 'that traytour, Deeth'. 'See ye that ook?' is the line that popped into my mind. Under the oak tree, death awaits.) Side effects included vomiting and diarrhoea. But of course they are side effects to many pills. They are the possible side effects of almost every pill Bo takes – five or six different tablets every day.

Bo felt okay. He ate some lunch, drank some tea. I telephoned our son Olaf, and told him Bo wasn't well and that I had to go out. He asked when I had to go. Five o'clock. I won't be home until late, maybe midnight.

We were still at the stage where time mattered. Little bits of time; events that would soon seem unspeakably trivial still mattered. We were in ordinary time, the place where we live, when it mattered whether Olaf would have time to get back to his flat that night. When it mattered that I would have time to get my hair blow-dried, to buy sweets for Halloween callers. We were still in ordinary time, the clock ticking, the diary full of appointments, each prefixed by its time. Launch 6.30 p.m. (or should that be 7?). Concert 7.30 p.m. (but you can arrive at the interval, i.e. 9). Hairdresser 2.30 p.m.

I went to my hairdresser, then to Tesco where I bought lots of bags of sweets for the trick or treaters. At ten to five, Olaf was on the doorstep.

'Not sure what Bo will eat,' I said.

'Okay,' he said. 'I'll do something.'

Olaf is very quiet, and does not use words lightly. He is totally reliable, very, very kind. Many times, I have called on him to stay with Bo, while I am out doing something. He and Nadezhda, his partner (now wife), have always come. For an evening, for a weekend. She comes all smiles, he comes silently, they never complain or fuss. I had no qualms about saying goodbye to Bo. By now we were very friendly again. Bo was tired and a bit queasy but none of the terrible side effects had occurred. I guessed he would be all right in a day or two.

'Drink a lot of water,' I said.

Did I kiss him goodbye? Maybe.

Somehow I thought water would dilute the impact of the pills. I had read that they were slow release so I was still a bit worried.

I headed off. The launch was great – a very enthusiastic event, for Brenda, who had a huge circle of friends and family. It was her first book, people had been hearing about it for a long time, and were delighted that it had come to fruition. Her daughter had composed a piece of music for the occasion, which she played on the harp. I gave my talk, about Samhain. This is the night when the dead and the fairies come out to wander on earth. It is a dangerous night, when the dead walk the earth and you may meet a ghost. It is also the season of storytelling …

All this, I said, and much more, and everyone clapped, and told me it was wonderful.

I grabbed a few sandwiches – how lucky there is food, I said, to Kelly Fitzgerald, who had introduced me to Brenda, but who was also rushing to Liberty Hall and the concert.

Liberty Hall was packed with people. I crept into the back

of the balcony and listened to what remained of the first half of the concert. Many brilliant traditional musicians and singers. Vincent Woods and Doireann Ní Bhriain were introducing it, with a mixture of warmth and professionalism. I was impressed by their ability to come up with some appropriate, often witty, comment, after every performance.

At the interval, I tried to find the green room. As I wandered around the foyer, I met some people from the audience – Maj O Catháin, for instance, who asked if Bo was there.

'He's not feeling very well,' I said, lightly, realising that it sounded like a white lie.

Eventually I went backstage, where a festive atmosphere prevailed – bottles of beer and wine, many young people running around, waiting to go on or off. The buzz was infectious. I remembered how it felt, putting on plays, which I had done long ago in the 1990s. The excitement of the theatre, the sense of purpose, of total commitment to the show, the pleasurable pressure of all that. I found myself, though, left alone in a dressing room, and I wondered where everyone was – I didn't realise there were several dressing rooms and I had landed in the first, outer one. I read over my script, made some last-minute revisions, as I always do.

I phoned Olaf from the green room. Bo was feeling 'a bit queasy', he said, using a phrase that would be repeated several times over the next week. He had eaten some supper but vomited it up.

('If he gets sick take him to the hospital.')

Now he was asleep. Too preoccupied to feel more than mildly uneasy, I told Olaf to go home, that everything would be all right.

Eventually, at 10.30, it was my turn – I had been preceded by the Swords Mummers, so colourful and otherworldly in their magnificent straw costumes. Vincent said a few words about the Urban Folklore Project, introduced me, and I stood at the podium and delivered my brief talk. I could not see the audience – the auditorium was black, and I was flooded in light. But they laughed at my jokes and I got that sense of rapport you can get, from the stage. I introduced my first recording, which was of Lyrics Murphy, a man I collected from in Ringsend – by coincidence, I had first met Lyrics on another Halloween night, long ago in 1979. I gave a rather full introduction to this astonishing man, who had been passionately interested in his home, Ringsend, and had under his own steam documented some of its lore, especially its vast range of nicknames. I had been instructed to nod to the light box up at the back to give them to cue to play the recording.

'And now we'll listen to Lyrics Murphy,' I said and raised my head and hand to the box. 'Talking about nicknames in Ringsend.'

The voice of a woman, from Black Pitts, describing midwives and childbirth, flooded the vast theatre.

Another glitch.

The audience didn't seem to mind. Once they realised what was happening, they listened to Rosanna O'Reilly – who was colourful and hilarious – and gave themselves to the moment. I apologised, although it was not my fault – or was it? I should have insisted on a rehearsal. But how could I have done that? Where would I have got the time, on that hectic day? I should have come home from Donegal earlier. But. But. Many ifs and buts.

As soon as I was finished, feeling deflated – because no matter how minor a glitch is, it is deflating, and one feels like an idiot, and one wishes it hadn't happened – I dashed across to Tara Street DART station to catch the train home. I just missed one, and had to wait for almost half an hour – this long wait always feels like an eternity at that hour of the night. When the train came, it was a two-carriage train. Drat, I thought, now I probably won't even get a seat. But I did.

I sat in the corner, opposite a tall man with a head of curly grey hair. He looked rather thespian, like a Shakespearian actor. Although I was very tired, I opened my Kindle and began to read – I have many books on my Kindle and I chose a short story by Margaret Drabble, a comfort read for me, since I knew this would pass the time easily, and absorb me just enough to keep me interested on the trip home. The train journey from the city centre to Shankill takes about forty minutes, which is long enough, especially if you've been waiting for half an hour for the train. At night it always feels much longer.

After a while the man opposite spoke.

'Excuse me,' he said in a refined voice. A bit Englishy. 'Is that a Kindle?'

I confirmed that it was.

We conversed for the rest of the journey home. I had a moment's hesitation – I knew I could return to my reading and he would respect that. But I decided he was not a dangerous man who was planning to rob/rape/murder me as soon as I got off the train. Also, he was educated. He knew something about literature – he had been a friend of Francis Stuart and advised me to read all of his work. I have read *Black List, Section H,* more than once, and liked it, but had a hazy memory of it.

The man was still on the train when I got off, so I guessed he lived in Bray, and wondered who he was. I thought, we may see him at the Mermaid – Bo and I sometimes went to the Mermaid Arts Centre in Bray on Monday nights, when they show a movie, from some group called European Film Art. We always met people we know, on those Monday nights, which we enjoyed very much. We'd been there just a few weeks before, although the last movie we had seen was Woody Allen's *Blue Jasmine*, in the cinema in Dún Laoghaire. We never missed a Woody Allen movie.

When I got home, it was after midnight. Bo was asleep and didn't wake when I slipped into bed beside him. It was nice and warm there, as always, and I curled up safely and fell asleep.

DAY 3

'Yesterday'

Bo's flat was L-shaped. The foot of the L had big windows at both ends, so got plenty of light. There was a kitchen at one end, and a sitting area with a fireplace at the other. In the leg of the L was the rest of the sitting room, where the blue sofa was. The wall facing the sofa was shelved from floor to ceiling and full of books. Two bedrooms, the bigger one of which was the 'library', also filled from floor to ceiling with books, and had a large handsome desk in the middle. Bo's typewriter, his containers for pens and pencils and paper clips and things, neatly arranged. An Anglepoise lamp. The smaller bedroom was his bedroom. It contained a single bed. All the rooms had windows so the flat was bright. Somehow it seemed too small nevertheless, but that was probably owing to the books that filled every spare bit of wall. Any bit of wall you could see was painted white. There was a blue carpet and deep ochre-coloured curtains. Bo had chosen the carpet and the curtains himself and they reflected his taste: he liked blue, deep yellow ochre, terracotta. At this time, I assumed he had very definite tastes, knew exactly how to choose furniture and everything else. He was the professor; he had knowledge and authority. Although he was reserved, and sometimes said he was shy, he was one of the most lively, confident, and vivacious people I had ever known and he was never at a loss for words.

*

I didn't feel like going in to work the next morning. Both Bo and I were in holiday mood: we had moved into a new time zone, the time of love, where the clock, that governed life in the library, in work, had no role to play. We'd moved into a mood that transcended time.

Besides, I was dressed in my fine frock and jacket. It was not unusual to dress well in the National Library – actually, it was expected – but in this new frock I would feel over the top. Also, the thought of travelling in from Booterstown frightened me. What if I met a colleague on the bus? Several of the librarians lived along the coast in south Dublin. Everyone knew I lived in Rathmines and would smell a rat if they spotted me on a bus from Blackrock. Everyone in the world was watching me and judging me.

Sex with Bo was different from anything I had experienced before. He was patient, and amused, and generous. Unlike anyone I had ever met, unlike me, he regarded sex as perfectly normal and natural. Nobody who had been brought up in Ireland during the 1960s could possibly be without sexual hang-ups. Any sex education that existed was designed to terrify you. No doubt some people managed to ignore the dire warnings, to grow up unscathed, although one wonders how they could manage this. But biddable people, good learners, good students, are influenced by what they are taught. Messages were mixed in the 1970s. We knew Philip Larkin's poem about the sexual revolution:

> *Sexual intercourse began*
> *In nineteen sixty-three*
> *(which was rather late for me) –*
> *Between the end of the 'Chatterley' ban*
> *And the Beatles' first LP.*

Sexual intercourse didn't begin in Ireland in 1963, however, and attitudes were very muddled.

For Bo, sex was a pleasure to which anyone was entitled if they wanted it, like food or drink or walking in the woods. It was a normal part of any loving relationship. I had been trained in celibacy, and in the expectation that loving relationships with men could be maintained, for years, without sexual intercourse. Probably many marriages in Ireland avoided it too. In the absence of contraception, abstinence was the only real form of birth control. What a country! The rules of the tribe were absorbed from the rules of Catholicism. Patriarchal, puritanical and in many instances simply daft, they were translated into iron conventions and taboos, and into the law of the land.

Sexual intercourse was not the only sort of communication that was severely restricted in Ireland in 1978. Telephone connections were also limited, although not, of course, illegal. Bo had applied for a telephone when he bought his apartment but the waiting list was three years' long. So he wouldn't get a phone until 1981, at the earliest. He had a telephone at work. If he needed to make a phone call when the department was closed he had to make do with the public telephone box. These green and cream boxes were situated here and there around the city. There was one halfway down Booterstown Avenue where the pub and the shops were, and there was a phone in the hall of the pub. The phones were coin phones: you inserted some money – sixpence for a local call – into a slot, dialled the number. When someone answered the call, you pressed Button A, and then they could hear you. The call lasted for five minutes and then you had to top it up with another sixpence.

If nobody answered your call, you could press Button B, and your money would be returned, rattling noisily into a little black steel pocket.

Often, the buttons got stuck and neither Button A nor Button B worked.

I decided to call the library, and tell them I was not feeling well and was taking a half-day. The regulation was that you had to call in sick on the morning of your sick leave, which was reasonable if you had a phone in your house, but difficult if you didn't have one. Of course if, as in this case, you weren't actually sick, it wasn't a huge imposition to run out and make the call from the coin box. The one on Booterstown Avenue wasn't broken. I got through to Maurice, who was understanding.

I had breakfast with Bo in the breakfast nook. He had instant coffee, and sliced pan.

'Would you like an egg?'

No.

'Cornflakes?'

No.

'What would you like?' he laughed, exasperated.

'I usually eat toast.'

He didn't have a toaster, but he made toast on the grill on the electric stove.

He seemed younger now, in the morning, moving around the little kitchen, which was too small for him. It was not that he was such a big man. Six foot – taller than many Irishmen but not outrageously tall. And he was slender enough, eighty-two kilos, just the right weight for his height, according to himself. But he was a man who seemed bigger than he was. His voice was big and round and deep. His character filled up spaces, and needed lots of room. In big rooms with high ceilings, he seemed to fit comfortably. In this kitchen in a small flat in Booterstown, he looked like a giant in a doll's house.

Our conversation risked being awkward, now that the evening was over. Before, when we had talked together we were discussing my thesis, or he was telling me about something he had read, advising me to read this or read that. We weren't used to small talk and I wasn't used to taking the initiative in conversation. My habit was to let other people do the talking and I would respond. The glow of the sunshine and our post-coital intimacy kept the conversation from being strained, but only just.

After breakfast, I decided to return home, to change and go to work in the afternoon.

He hugged me tightly.

'When will you come back?'

'I don't know.'

'How about this evening?'

His eyes sparkled and he smiled broadly.

Yes.

All Saints' Day

Next morning, Friday, one week after our drive to Gweedore, Bo stayed in bed. I gave him some tea and dry toast, which he ate. He told me he felt a bit queasy – that word again – but not too bad. It did not occur me to call the doctor – when do you call the doctor? When someone is at death's door? Who do you call when someone is not well enough to go to the doctor but not sick enough to go to hospital?

Neither Bo nor I wanted to go to the A&E in our local hospital, Loughlinstown, or in Vincent's. We hate Loughlinstown but it's just down the road. It's handy. And everyone hates the thought of the alternative, which is Vincent's A&E: huge, crowded, you'd be on a trolley for days. How many Irish people die because they can't stand the thought of the A&E?

I went into Belfield where I had a workshop at eleven. It went on till one, and I planned to stay on for a few hours, but I felt anxious and decided to go home.

Bo was very tired, still in bed, still nauseated. The diarrhoea that had started the day before continued and he said there was nothing left in him, he felt drained. He ate a little toast and tea, however, and that stayed down. I went to the local shop and bought some natural yoghurt, which is supposed to be good for upset stomachs. I dropped into the pharmacy, bought some Imodium, to counteract the diarrhoea, and some anti-inflammatories for Bo's gout, since he would no longer be taking the tablets that had been originally prescribed for him.

The diarrhoea stopped. Bo had a little food – scrambled egg, toast – and felt a bit better. Did he get up that night? I think so. I think he may have come downstairs for a while. But I can't remember.

DAY 4

Babette's Feast

Bo was teaching me Danish, in preparation for the year ahead in Copenhagen. Not for a moment did he suggest that I shouldn't go.

'You'll go to Denmark. You'll finish your thesis. And then we'll get married.'

There was no question in either of our minds. We had already come so far, taken such risks, in four days. Of course we would marry. He was my professor, I was his student. He had been in love with me for a year and I had been half in love with him for two or three years. He didn't propose, but he talked of the marriage as if it were a done deal, and showed me the kind of house we might live in. A big house with steep gables, mock-Tudor timbering, off the Stillorgan Road. We passed it as we walked to Belfield – we even walked to Belfield sometimes, in the sunny May mornings. When half the world would see us from the 46A bus.

'It's very big.' I couldn't imagine living in such a house, or in any house. I couldn't really imagine being married either, in spite of my lifelong ambition to acquire that status. The wedding was the goal, and my imaginings ended there, just where all the fairy tales stopped.

Anyway, although everyone I knew wanted to get married, I was still very conscious of the social rules, the whispered constitution, about who you should marry – you could only marry someone of the opposite sex; you could only marry someone who was single or a widower; you could only marry someone who was a Catholic. You could only marry someone who was roughly the same age as yourself. Some clauses of the whispered constitution were also in the real constitution, the law of the land.

I would only marry someone I was in love with.

Bo satisfied my own main requirement. I was in love with him. I respected him. He was a good match for me and I could spend my life with him. But he did not fit the bill of ideal spouse, as far as the conventions of Ireland were concerned. Marrying the professor might be viewed as a bit of a coup in college. But outside that hermetically-sealed world the age difference would cause general disapproval, even mockery. Was there not a folk custom involving communal sneering at May-December matches? Charivari? The neighbours came to the house on the wedding night and rattled buckets or dustbin lids or something to express their disapproval.

When my thoughts wandered along these lines it was as if all Bo's other attributes – his lovely voice, his brilliance, his handsome body – were cancelled out by his age. I was terrified of what other people thought. I wanted universal approval. Far from being an Arctic explorer, I was a coward. I think I had been brought up to be a coward, trained to want to please everybody, with no sense of rebelling and pleasing myself.

I wanted to be with Bo forever and apparently he felt the same about me. But I couldn't think of it as a reality. Anyway, we had been together for just a few weeks. In Ireland, nobody got married after a few weeks, except for one reason. You got married when you had served your time going to the pictures for a couple of years, working and saving for a deposit on a house. You got married, in Dublin, when you had taken out a mortgage and chosen a semi-detached in the suburbs. Marriage and house ownership went together like a horse and carriage. In the referendums in Ireland over the next thirty years, the reactionaries would claim, again and again, that marriage was all about a man, a woman and children. But everyone who got an engagement ring knew that marriage was about a man, a woman and a mortgage.

Bo and I were not going to buy a house right now. But he was thinking ahead. And he longed to get out of that little flat, where there wasn't enough room for him – or for his books. I, on the other hand, rather liked the flat: the cosiness of it, the sense of being in a little nest of books – and television. We watched *Dallas* together, on Saturday evenings.

For an hour, every time we met, we had a Danish lesson. Bo gave me a copy of *Babettes Gaestebud* (*Babette's Feast*), in Danish translation. Karen Blixen, who was Danish, wrote this story originally in English, the language she had learned in Kenya. It is said that she wrote it because a friend advised her that if she wanted to be successful in the United States she should write about food. Later she translated her own story to her native Danish; that's the version we read. We read about half a page, at first, and as time went on a page or more. It's a novella, rather than a short story or a novel, so it was a good choice for the time at our disposal – six weeks – before Bo would leave Dublin for the summer house in Kerry, to which he longed to go. Nothing would disturb his plans for the summer months in Dunquin. Not love or marriage or me. This was a bit of shock, but one I would get used to.

I didn't know a word of Danish, so we were starting from scratch. He read a sentence aloud, in an exaggerated Danish accent. (He was a Swede; the languages are very closely related, but Swedish sounds quite different from Danish and Swedes tend to think that Danish sounds laughable. The glottal stop which is characteristic of Danish is especially strange, until you get used to it. It is true that Danish doesn't sound as musical as Swedish, but it has its own charm. Later I realised that of the Scandinavian languages, Danish is the most useful one to start with. When you have mastered the Danish phonetics, it's fairly easy to understand the much clearer pronunciation and accents of the Swedes and the Norwegians.) Then he would translate it, word by word, and explain the grammar as we went.

Det bodde engang ved siden af en laenge snaever fjord I Norge två søstrer ... Once upon a time two sisters lived by the side of a long narrow fjord in Norway.

Love is the best teacher. I loved the text and the teacher, so I learnt fast and well.

After the first day, I prepared for the lessons by trying to translate, at home with the dictionary. I had to look up every single word, and I listed them all with translations at the back of the little book. In pencil – Bo would never deface a book, any book, in any way. His library was a working library, containing books he was interested in for their content – folklore, Irish literature, Icelandic literature, Swedish literature, anthropology, classics, and much else. He was not a collector as such or a bibliophile who bought books for their dates, their value, or their bindings. But he was an obsessive book buyer. And he had a fine bibliophilic sensibility. The pages and the bindings were the bodies that contained the souls of the books and he respected them.

I was much more careless. Dog-ears never bothered me – my mother had showed me how to make them when I was a child of seven – and I occasionally used a biro to underline something if I couldn't find a pencil. And I was the kind of person who could never find a pencil, whereas Bo had a few in his breast pocket at all times, and a few on his bedside locker, and a dozen in a special container, made for him by his mother, on his big desk.

Danish is not a very difficult language for an English speaker. It's a Germanic language, like English, so many of the words have a familiar ring to them. *Mand* for man. *Maelk* for milk. *Hus* for house. And so on. The grammar too is not so different. Nouns and adjectives are gendered, and nouns and adjectives and articles agree, which is a bit more complicated than English, but it's not a highly inflected language – less inflected than

German, or Icelandic, and much less than say Finnish or Irish or Bulgarian. The thing that seemed very odd was that the article came after the noun, tacked on to it – *manden* instead of the man. If the article came in front, it was indefinite – *en mand,* a man. *En barn*, a child. *Barnen*, the child. The same system applies in Swedish and Norwegian and Icelandic (and in other unrelated languages, such as Bulgarian). Bo was surprised that I found this strange. It was so natural to him that he didn't see the problem. And after a few weeks I got quite used to it and did not see it either.

The Danish lessons gave our meetings a purpose, apart from kissing and making love and having dinner. They put our relationship back on the familiar footing, student and teacher, and as a result we were totally at ease with one another. My progress delighted me. The new language unfolded in front of my eyes, step by step, word by word; I was learning to read it, with a beloved teacher to guide me. Our life together would involve many ordinary aspects, but this aspect, teaching and learning, was at its heart. In these hours we were most at peace, most ourselves.

For the first week we met every day, and for the second, every second day. Sometimes Bo had engagements in the evening, or work that he could not put off. I had nothing to do except go to work during the day and 'work on my thesis', an ongoing task that was already becoming a chore rather than an exploration. Since breaking up with Oliver I hadn't cultivated new friendships to any extent. During the two or three years I had been with him, we had spent most of our time in one another's company. Parties and group activities we had attended together, the way young couples, married or not, do. After the break-up, it had surprised me to notice that some people who had been mutual acquaintances dropped me while continuing their friendship with Oliver. I supposed he was more interesting, more promising. And he was male, which gave him status I simply couldn't have in the academic circles we moved in. In 1978, the Irish academic world was completely, and completely unconsciously, biased in favour of men. The vast majority of lecturers and professors in UCD were male, although in the Faculty of Arts a majority of students were women. Nobody seemed to find this state of affairs in the least bit anomalous – although they would, quite soon.

On the evenings when I was not seeing Bo, I sat in my bedsitter and translated chunks of *Babettes Gaestebud*. I placed myself on an armchair by the long sash window, open to the air. Outside in the garden a huge chestnut tree flaunted its fresh spring green leaves, growing bigger almost by the minute, and its cones of creamy blossoms. The evening sun bathed the weathered slate roofs of the sweet old brick houses; light traffic hummed a soothing melody on its way from Rathmines to Harold's Cross.

I looked up the words in my Gyldendal's red dictionary and slowly, like ice melting, the symbols on the page were transformed into a story I could understand, people I began to know, a place that grew familiar, word by word, line by line, page by page. A new country, a new language, new people. On the evenings with Bo, I was beginning to know him, his past, his country, his people, and on the other evenings I was beginning to know Denmark.

No Swedish, as yet. Bo's own language – it was close to Danish, but one thing at a time.

My worries about what other people would think had faded, or I had pushed them away. Anyway, since we had told nobody about our relationship for the moment they didn't think anything. Besides, we were now in a cocoon of love, in a private world that transcended everything else. When I was away from the flat I walked on air. The world around me – Rathmines with its red library building on the corner, the bridge over the sparkling waters of the Grand Canal – shimmered and sparkled and I walked with a light step everywhere. Magical, magical, the month of May played a bright and lovely tune wherever I went. My eyes were aglow, my heart was light. The ordinary world of work, family, community, the streets, the customers in the library, the catalogues to be checked, had become the unreal world. The real world was the story I escaped into – the work on that book – by the long, elegant window in the light of evening, and the flat I escaped into with Bo, that little space filled with books and with Bo himself, his voice, his laugh, his bear hug when I arrived at six o'clock.

It was a time out of time. A summer of love.

D-Day

On Saturday morning Bo was in much better form. He stayed in bed, enjoyed having breakfast there, and read. I brought over the radio from its shelf so he could listen to music if he wanted to. It was a bright sunny day and we both felt happy – it looked as if this particular crisis was over. The three pills were obviously well out of his system, he was smiling, his natural cheerful self.

At about three o'clock I went to the shopping centre in Carrickmines, to buy a new laptop. My old one was held together with Sellotape, and I had been promising to get a replacement for several months. I thought, this is the one thing I will do today, and then this problem will be solved for once and for all. I spent about an hour, perhaps an hour and a half, away from home, and in Currys I bought the laptop I am now using, from a very helpful salesman, who sold me quite a lot of additional bits and bobs – some are still in a bag somewhere in my bedroom, unused: they never will be. He kept the laptop, to install some sort of recovery programme on to it, and I was to collect it the following day, in the afternoon.

When I got home Bo was on the floor of our bedroom, in a corner at the opposite side from the door. He was prostrate, his pyjamas were wet, and he could not get up.

'What happened?'

'I don't know, I don't know. I have wet my pants, I am incontinent.'

'You're not incontinent. That can happen to anyone. How did you get over here?'

I wondered if he had had a stroke. I did the checks you are supposed to do in these circumstances. His voice was normal. His eyes were normal. He could raise his arms. I did not think he had had a stroke.

I considered calling the ambulance. But the ambulance takes you to the local hospital, which is run-down and crowded. The last place Bo or I wanted him to be was that hospital.

I tried to help him up. But he couldn't get up. I could not understand it.

I made a terrible mistake here. I should have called the ambulance, no matter where it would have taken him. This was a critical moment and I fluffed it. If I had known about private ambulances I would have called one. He could have been taken to the Blackrock Clinic. But I didn't know about them, and I couldn't get Bo into the car and drive him there. Like most people I have spoken to about this, I believed the only way you could get to Blackrock Clinic or the Beacon was under your own steam, in a car. There is a serious problem with the private hospitals in Ireland, which is that they have no emergency services – this is the case with the hospital Bo always attended, Vincent's Private – or very limited services, 9 to 5, Monday to Friday. The regular ambulance won't take you to the private hospitals, even if their emergency departments are open. There is an anomaly here, one more problem in the two-tier Irish health system. You can use your private hospital for consultations, operations, treatments that can be scheduled – but if you fall ill outside of office hours, you are likely to fall back into the public system.

I moved Bo close to the side of our bed, stopped trying to get him up – he was much too heavy – and made a bed for him on the floor. The fear of Loughlinstown was driving me, rather than concern for Bo or even for myself. Bo agreed that he didn't want to go to the local hospital and that we shouldn't call an ambulance.

He slept for a while on the floor, where he was comfortable. When he woke up he asked where am I? Then he got into bed, with some help from me. He slept, had some more tea and toast. He seemed to be okay. That night, I slept in the spare room next door in order not to disturb him. I did not know that I would never again sleep in the same bed as my husband, the bed we shared for almost thirty-one years.

Nordic walk

Sunday morning was sunny and fine. Bo was in good form again, cheerfully eating breakfast, reading. He got up and went to the bathroom. He was still a little 'queasy' but that was all. I was so sure he was on the mend that I thought about going for the hike I usually do on Sunday mornings with the Wicklow Nordic Walkers. But I decided not to and texted to cancel. Bo, in his warm optimistic voice, said, 'But you can go for a walk here. You can walk around the park.' Yes, I agreed, I would take a long walk on my way to get the Sunday papers.

I walked around Shanganagh Park, the walk Bo had loved over the past five or six years. He used to do it every single day – much more often than I did. A five or six kilometre walk. He was an institution in the neighbourhood, always with a cheery smile and hello for everyone. Two years ago, when his backache became very bad, he had to stop taking this very long walk. But he continued to go up and down Corbawn Lane to buy the paper. He asked me not to accompany him – he was too slow, because of the pain, and he liked to go at exactly his own pace, a pace so slow that people often stopped to offer him a lift! It was at that point, two years ago, that I joined the Wicklow Nordic Walkers, since I could no longer go for long walks with Bo. Most weekends, I went for a hike with this group, in the grounds of

Kilruddery House or in the Wicklow mountains. I loved these walks, and the people in the group.

Bo was in fairly good form at lunchtime. I drove back to Carrickmines to collect my laptop, and spent about half an hour rooting through clothes in TK Maxx, considering a handbag. Then I suddenly became impatient with the shop and went home. Bo was tired, but decided to get up for dinner. Olaf came round, and we ate some confit of duck, which I had bought in Monaghan, at the duck farm at Emyvale, when we were driving back from Donegal. It was delicious. Bo only had some mashed potato, and did not eat more than a spoonful. He had ice cream, however, which he had been able to eat the day before as well. After dinner, Olaf went home, and Bo and I watched *Downton Abbey*, which we had missed the previous Sunday, in Magherawarden, and which we both enjoyed on this occasion.

We decided that Bo should sleep in the living room. This would save him the pain of going back upstairs. And I thought it would be convenient for him on Monday morning, when I teach, to be close to the kitchen. I was worried that he might fall again. I made up our sofa bed in the front room. The room was warm and cosy, with a fire dancing in the grate. In the morning, Bo would see the sun rising over the Irish Sea. The best view from our house is from that particular sofa – you see Dalkey Island, and Killiney Hill, whereas from the other front windows all you see is the Irish Sea, stretched out in front of you like yards of cloth in a haberdashery, sometimes blue, sometimes pewter, sometimes sparkling, sometimes angry. But plain. It is a plain sea, the sea that stretches in front of our house, with not much relieving its sea-ness.

Bo got into bed – actually he had not dressed, but come down in his dressing gown. It was just at this stage that he noticed a rash on his legs. He called me. The rash was very bad on his thighs, around his lower stomach, but there was also spotting on other parts of his body.

My first thought was that it was a reaction to the urine, which had dried on him, I realised, on Saturday. We had changed his pyjamas and washed his face and hands but not his legs or lower body. How could I have been so stupid? He has sensitive skin – on one occasion, at least, he, and one of our boys, broke out in a rash in reaction to a fabric softener. I searched around for some cream – Sudocrem, I knew, would be the right thing, if his was a nappy rash of sorts. But I had no Sudocrem. The only soothing thing I could find was aftersun cream, so I rubbed that into the affected areas. It gave some very temporary relief.

MONDAY

DAY 11,995

'See ye that ook?'

I went to bed upstairs, and Bo downstairs. In the morning, Monday morning, he said he had not slept well. The rash itched. I looked at him. The rash was much worse. It had spread everywhere. For some reason I thought it might be shingles and my heart sank. Shingles is very painful, if you are elderly, and lasts for a very long time.

I telephoned the doctor's surgery and told them what was wrong. I had to go teach my Monday morning class, I explained.

I just had to go. Missing a class was unthinkable.

But Bo was downstairs, he would let the doctor in.

This was our arrangement.

I went into college, taught two classes – oddly, I had the feeling they were the best classes I had ever taught, everything went so well, and I congratulated myself on being able to forget everything while I was teaching I've noticed on other occasions that this happens. I had an arrangement to meet a friend for lunch but I cancelled that and phoned Bo.

'The good news is that it's not shingles,' Bo said. 'The bad news is that I still have it, and the doctor is going to call back this evening. He's going to bring some cream for it. Sood ...'

'Sudocrem,' I said. 'I'll get some on the way.'

I rubbed Sudocrem all over the terrible red rash. It gave just momentary relief from the itch. By this time, it was about half past two. I don't remember much of what happened during that afternoon. Bo was reading *Bombi Bitt och Jag* – this is the book he had been reading over the weekend, an old children's book, a classic. He was almost finished but had twenty pages to go (he had read it many times before). Perhaps Bo slept. It is odd that I don't remember.

At about five, the doctor called. He looked at Bo's rash and speculated. It's from inside, he said. It's not a reaction to detergent or anything. An anti-viral medication will get rid of that. But what's causing it, that's the question.

At around this time Bo mentioned that he had not gone to the toilet – urinated – all day.

'When did you last go?'

Bo thought, that morning. But there was not very much.

The doctor looked at his tongue and said he was very dehydrated. He muttered that we should go to the hospital.

'They'll hydrate him, and get the kidneys functioning again. I'll call an ambulance.'

Does that mean Loughlinstown?

Or Vincent's?

'Bo's hospital is Vincent's Private. Can he go there?'

The doctor thought not. There is no A&E in Vincent's Private. He said we could go to the Blackrock Clinic if we drove ourselves, but they closed at six and it was already half past five. Besides, I knew Bo was in no condition to be taken to hospital by car.

I knew the system was two tier, unjust, and unegalitarian. But it wasn't the moment for me to protest about the injustice of the Irish healthcare system. I didn't think Loughlinstown was appropriate, for Bo (or anyone). Last time he was there, in an emergency, he was in a ward with six people, one of whom played the radio loudly all day without pause. The treatment he got on that occasion was fine – that is to say, it worked. But the conditions were dreadful: noisy, somewhat chaotic, bad washing facilities.

'Listen. They'll hydrate Bo this evening. You'll be picking him up tomorrow and taking him home.'

I knew that you can never be sure about the future.

He reassured me. 'You can get him transferred out of Loughlinstown if he's there for longer than a day. People do that all the time.'

'So?' I looked at Bo.

We decided: Loughlinstown.

I was thinking, it will be handier than Vincent's. The queue in the A&E won't be so long. It'll be easy to collect Bo there tomorrow.

The doctor rang for the ambulance, then sat down and wrote a long letter, laboriously. An hour passed. I felt sorry for him – still with a patient at the end of a long day. I asked if he needed to be here when the ambulance came and he said no. He told me to give the letter to the ambulance men, and he also asked me to move my car out of the drive, so it would be easy for them to wheel the trolley up to the door.

At about seven o'clock the ambulance arrived.

'Here goes!' I said to Bo, who was in the sofa bed.

Two large, cheerful men came into the room. I handed them the letter.

'I can't read the handwriting!' one of them said, stuffing it in his pocket.

'Come on, my good man!' he said to Bo. 'Off we go.'

'Bo can't walk very well,' I said. 'He fell earlier today.'

'We'll help you!'

Looking bewildered, and frightened, Bo sat at the side of the bed. I put on his dressing gown. The ambulance man put on his slippers.

'Now! We're all set! Up you go!'

Bo struggled to his feet.

Why didn't I protest more vigorously? I was bewildered too. I had already forgotten that I'd moved the car so they could wheel Bo down the drive.

With a huge amount of support from the men, Bo, in his dressing gown and slippers, walked out of the house and down the drive to the ambulance. It reminded me of Jesus Christ walking up Calvary, and indeed it was soon to bear more resemblance to that.

'I'll follow in the car,' I said.

'Or you can come in the ambulance if you like.'

'But I'll need to get back from the hospital.'

'We won't be taking you back,' he joked.

One of them put Bo on a small seat, in the back of the ambulance. He looked very pale, very sick, and shocked.

They checked his blood pressure.

A voice from the machine, a female voice, said 'CPR, CPR, CPR.'

The men glanced at one another. Bo was clearly in deep shock. They moved him from the chair to the bed in the ambulance, covered him with a blanket. They didn't give him CPR, but they raised his feet and lowered his head, and some of his colour returned.

'You don't bother coming up to the hospital for an hour, love. Or two hours. They're really busy up there. Nothing will happen for hours.'

'Thanks,' I said. I kissed Bo and said I'd see him soon.

I decided to go to the hospital immediately. I packed a small bag with some of Bo's things – clothes, two books he had asked me to bring. I got a few books for myself – I was reading a new novel, to review for *The Irish Times*, so I grabbed that and a Swedish novel from the Swedish book club I belong to.

My car – our car, but since Bo didn't drive we tended to refer to it as the car, or my car – was parked on the road, not in the drive. When I went out, my next-door neighbour, Janice, was coming out of her house. She asked me if Bo was all right. She had seen the ambulance. She gave me a big hug and said not to worry. Susan, another neighbour, also passed. I explained what had happened. It's nothing, I said. It's just a precaution. But, to

Bo, aged about twenty

Bo and I, waiting to get married

Our wedding, Uppsala, Sweden, 1982

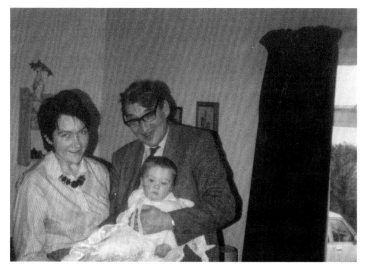

Bo and I with our son Olaf

With Bo's sister Vera in Uppsala

With our two sons at Olaf's First Communion, 1992.
From left to right: me, Olaf, Bo and Ragnar.

Bo lecturing, UCD, 1990s

Bo and a storyteller

In Iceland, 1991

Bo in his library, 2012

Bo, *c.* 2000

Donegal, 1990s

Islandbridge, 2013

my surprise, I burst into tears.

'The ambulance is scary,' Susan said.

'Yes, very scary.'

That was it, I thought. The ambulance is scary. That must be why I'm crying.

But I remembered Bo, walking down the drive in his slippers and dressing gown, and his white disbelieving face in the ambulance.

I drove to the hospital, paid the parking fee, and went into A&E.

The A&E waiting room in Loughlinstown has gradually deteriorated over the years I have been going there. When we first began, soon after we married and moved to our house by the sea, I was frequently up in that hospital with our baby and toddler sons – when they fell; when Ragnar swallowed (as I thought) a piece of glass; when he was bitten by a dog. I remember it as, first, rather basic; then it got renovated and painted and looked modern and cheerful. There were some toys for children, and magazines on a table. It was not a great place but it was normal.

The last time I was here was in March, when Bo came in with a minor complaint. ('You'll be out today, just get them to check it,' the doctor had said.) On that occasion Bo was in for three or four days. I later heard from a nurse that the ward he had been in was the worst ward in the place, which is saying a lot. Then the waiting room looked different from when I'd seen it last, in the 1990s, probably. It was just an alcove in a corridor, extremely shabby, with three or four rows of plastic seats. No table, no toys, no magazines, not a single gesture towards comfort. I had noticed then, and I noticed again now, that no middle-class people were in the waiting room. I am not saying this in any mood of snobbery. But it was plain that anyone who knew better or who could afford better went elsewhere. This was a hospital for the poor, and the HSE (Health Service Executive) provided them with the sort of waiting room and accommodation it apparently believes they deserve: a grim, grey place without the slightest pretension to comfort or cheerfulness. A hospital like this could not exist in Sweden, where Bo came from. Such places, if they ever existed, have probably not been in Sweden since the before the Second World War.

Trying to be positive – he'd be home tomorrow anyway – I asked at reception for Bo. He was admitted about fifteen minutes ago, I said. He came in an ambulance.

The man at the desk looked at the computer. 'No, he's not here,' he said.

'The ambulance said they were taking him here.'

'No, nobody by that name.'

He rang someone, spoke for a few moments, and then turned back to me. 'No. When did the ambulance leave? Where do you live? They must have gone to Vincent's.'

My heart lifted slightly. Already, now that I was reminded of what this place was like, I knew he would be better off in Vincent's. The A&E here was obviously very busy anyway – the main reason we had for coming here no longer existed.

'I'll ring Vincent's,' he said. 'Are you …?'

'His wife.'

Then someone came into the reception area.

'Is your husband a professor?' she asked.

'Yes, yes,' I said.

'Ah, he's here all right. Come this way.'

Bo was on a trolley in a small room, off the main A&E. At least he was in a bed of sorts, and on his own. He looked not too bad. I was very glad to see him.

'They told me you weren't here!'

'They don't listen to what I say,' he said.

We laughed.

Nobody had done anything.

Why weren't they hydrating him? What were they waiting for?

'Are you thirsty?'

Yes, he was.

I bought a bottle of water from a vending machine in the corridor – there seemed to be no water supply in the hospital, for patients – and he sipped it.

An hour passed.

A nurse came, and inserted a system tube into Bo's arm.

'I have to take bloods,' he said. 'And I am giving him something for the rash. Then the doctor will look at the results and see. What is the matter with him?'

They talked about Bo as if he didn't exist.

'The doctor has written an account.'

'Oh, where is that?'

'The ambulance man had it.'

He looked in a file.

'Difficult handwriting!' he said.

I told him that Bo had a rash and was dehydrated. He nodded.

'The doctor will come when he is ready,' he said.

I settled in the chair beside Bo and read my novel. Bo dozed off – it was cold in the room so I covered him with my coat and his dressing gown.

About three hours later a young doctor came in.

The questions started again.

'Why didn't they put in a drip?' he said, shaking his head in irritation.

'That's what I was wondering,' I said. He didn't respond.

Bo, who had come into this hospital to be hydrated, had lain for four hours without even a glass of water being supplied.

'We'll keep him tonight,' the doctor said. 'I will get a drip inserted. His sodium levels are low.' He mentioned electrolytes, a word I had heard for the first time on Thursday, when the doctor as the medical centre had said something about magnesium levels, electrolytes, and other things that could be affected by the medication.

The doctor asked the nurse if they had sodium which could be given orally. No.

'We'll X-ray him and admit him,' he said.

It was almost midnight.

'Will that happen soon?'

'As soon as we have a bed.'

I felt reassured, as I always do when I talk to a doctor, especially a young doctor: he was intelligent, everything he said was sensible, he seemed honest ('Why didn't they put in a drip?'). Bo was in good hands.

It was very late, and I decided to go home. I had an interview with a radio producer in the morning. I was going to talk about 'The Children of Lir', for a programme on storytelling. It seemed important to me to keep this appointment. Bo was in a shabby, old hospital, but he was in a hospital. They would keep him for the night. I could come and collect him tomorrow after the interview and take him home and normal life would resume.

Bo's rash seemed to be getting better. It was no longer very itchy. I kissed him goodnight and told him I'd see him the following day.

DAY 26

Breaking the spell

It was I who broke the spell. Stupidly. But spells of magic, spells of great joy must always break eventually, just like spells of sunny weather. These months of pure bliss – for this was our one true honeymoon, when it came to the crunch – must always come to an end. We can't sustain a mood of high excitement, perfect happiness, for very long. After a month I needed to escape from it, just as you need to throw out the Christmas tree and all the lustrous sparkle that goes with it, and move again in plain rooms. Or as you may wish, for an unaccountable perverse moment, to return to the chill banality of foggy autumn workdays, even as you stroll around an ancient white village on a Greek island, drenched in eternal summer. Too much happiness hurts your eyes. We can sustain grief and sadness for considerably longer than joy, oddly enough.

I didn't know this, then, when I was twenty-four. You can take more bright lights and rich sunshine when you're young, you think warm days will never cease. But I had already suspected that Bo would not be able to sustain his level of euphoria. I liked to think of myself as a calm individual. I believed I could keep a rein on myself, even when I was flying high, or racing down a ski slope at a hundred miles an hour.

Bo's emotions ran higher and faster than mine. He was more excitable. He was like a child with a wonderful new toy – love, I think, rather than me as such.

Slow down, you move too fast, I had been thinking. But how can you ask an enthusiastic child to slow down, to dampen their joy? It would be like waking a dreaming toddler from a delicious sleep. Or, perhaps, like forcing a toddler who is delirious with the joy of playing to stop and go to bed.

For years Bo had been suffering loss. The end of his marriage had hurt him deeply. When you're young, even when you are as young or as old as forty-three, the only way to fall out of love with the person who is lost is to fall in love with someone else. I knew that much, as every twenty-four-year-old who has loved and lost knows it. There's just one really effective cure for a broken heart.

No wonder he was on top of the world. Bo, whose capacity for optimism and enthusiasm, whose love of life was greater than anyone's – although the life he loved was not the common one, but encompassed, as well as nature and people and food and music and ordinary fun, knowledge, learning, the life of the mind. He had the capacity for boundless joy, and his character was tempered by pain and loss. But I suspected that he couldn't stay on top of the world, where the oxygen is thin, although the snow and the air are glittering, for very long. I didn't know about manic depression, or bipolar disorder, and Bo did not suffer from these conditions. But there was something – some capacity or tendency to be overexcited that made me uneasy. When will we meet again? Tonight! Let's buy that lovely big house on the corner, you'd like that. There was something not quite bearable in going so far, so fast. But maybe I was wrong. There was so much I didn't know about him. He was a stranger from a foreign land and a different generation. He seemed invulnerable, omniscient, sure of himself, and in ways he was. Maybe he could stay on the top of Mount Everest?

I myself pulled him down. I shattered our idyllic happiness as if it were a china bowl that I took from the cabinet and hurled against the floor.

Oliver had come round to talk to me. First it had seemed

like a friendly visit – he made enquiries about my plans to go to Denmark, which someone had told him about and which had taken him aback. When I told him about Bo and our relationship, he panicked. To make a long story short, he soon wanted me back. Breaking up had been a huge mistake.

Oliver became increasingly desperate. He couldn't sleep, he walked around Dublin at night, plagued by worries and regrets. He begged me to forgive him and resume our relationship.

In retrospect, it's easy to understand what was happening. Oliver and I had had a fairly long and serious relationship. But the romance had gone out of it for him, if it had ever been there, and had not been replaced by anything deeper. Now that I was involved with another man, whom he admired, I was once again the object of desire. All too often, we realise that we value someone when it's too late, when we've lost them. What we possess we take for granted. While I was alone, Oliver could assume, probably unconsciously, that I was available, still in love with him. But as soon as another man came on the scene, that presumption vanished. People, especially men, are competitive in love. The rival had to be displaced.

Oliver was a good person who genuinely believed that my relationship with Bo was a mistake. The prejudice against the age gap was universal. Bo was forty-five, but in Oliver's eyes he was about eighty. 'All he wants is a nursemaid!'

Why did I tell Bo about this?

Perhaps I hoped he would solve the problem? I could have solved it very easily myself, and very simply, and very obviously, by telling Oliver to get lost. Some young women must spend half their lives fending off admirers.

A more determined person, sure of her attractiveness and of her feelings, would have done just that. But I was not determined, and the return of Oliver had confused me. Three or four months ago I had been heartbroken. If he had come back at any time then I would have gladly gone back to him. But now I was in love with Bo. Or was I? What is love? What is infatuation, even?

It seems to be focused on one individual, to be a connection between two individuals. But the emotion is affected by third parties. Oliver did not love me when I was alone, and available, eager to be with him. Now it was obvious – he was not bluffing – that he believed he was very much in love with me because I was connected to Bo and not available.

What did I imagine Bo would feel when I told him all this? For a month he had been in love with a girl young enough to be his daughter, he had risked his reputation as a professor, he had promised to marry me. He was an entirely trustworthy and reliable man, and his trust had been betrayed. Again.

He dealt with the problem rationally.

'Well, dearest darling,' he said, opening his eyes and raising his eyebrows. 'You must decide between me and Oliver. I can't make up your mind for you.'

He spoke to me now like a teacher to a student. He was sitting at one side of the kitchen table and I at the other. It might have been his little desk in college.

'I love you,' I said.

The light was grey. It was a heavy June day, leaden.

'Yes, apparently,' he said. 'But I am old enough to be your father.' He sighed. 'We must remember that, when all is said and done.'

I, who had been full of joy, was full of tears.

TUESDAY

DAY 11,996

'The Children of Lir'

When I got home from the hospital, Gari, my neighbour on the other side, had left a message on the phone. She asked me to ring. 'It doesn't matter how late it is, just call. And if there is anything I can do, I will.'

Everyone else was more alarmed than I was. It was as if they had a premonition. But Bo would be home tomorrow. That's what the doctor had said.

I didn't call. It was almost one in the morning.

I got up at about seven and telephoned the hospital.

A nurse told me Bo had been a bit uneasy during the night but was sleeping. She told me I should see the doctor when I visited the hospital, and said visiting hours were between two and five. She said he would probably stay in hospital for the day. I told her I had something to do during the morning and would be in at two. I phoned Bo, who sounded okay. The rash had gone, he said. Great, I said, I'll see you later, around lunchtime.

Then.

I drove to Lake Derravaragh, near Multyfarnham, in County Westmeath.

The producer – her name was what? Emma? – wanted to

record the interview about 'The Children of Lir' in one of the places associated with them. The Children of Lir, Fionnuala and her three brothers, were transformed into swans by their stepmother, who had baulked at murdering them. Enchanted until a king's son from the north of Ireland married a king's daughter from the south of Ireland, they were banished to lonely places. They spent three hundred years at Lough Derravaragh, three hundred years in the Moyle, the stretch of water between Antrim and Scotland, and three hundred years at Lough Derg. Then they returned to Mayo, to Inis Guaire, where the spell was broken. Now nine hundred years old, they were baptised by St Maolaoise, and then died.

I had wondered about the point of going to Lough Derravaragh. Would it really make much difference where a radio interview was recorded? Perhaps the idea was that the place would enhance mood, inspire me in some intangible way? However, I felt reasonably happy, driving to Multyfarnham. I have visited Lough Derravaragh, always for very brief visits (by which I mean, about twenty minutes or half an hour) on several occasions since I first saw it fifteen years before. In 1998, Ragnar, our son, was attending a summer school in German, which was held in the boarding school in Multyfarnham. One Sunday, Bo and Olaf and I came to visit him – I was charmed by the old quaint village, and the smooth, flat lake. We had ice cream and coffee in the wooden cafe there – there was a caravan park on the edge of the lake, and I thought how nice it would be to have a caravan in this mythical and lovely place. Since then, on the way to or from Mayo, I have often made the detour and looked at the lake, usually with Bo. I was not sure when I was last there with him. Possibly as late as the previous February, when we were at the Merriman Winter School in Westport, and drove along this road, the M6.

Emma was waiting for me outside the church in Multyfarnham. We drove down to the lake, through trees like clouds of gold – such a perfect autumn that year after a perfect summer. The lake stretched, flat, gleaming under a blue sky through which the white cold clouds scudded. Reeds grew on the edge and in clumps, like islands, in the lake itself. There were four swans swimming on the waters, which lapped on the shore with a soothing, soft sound. That would be good, on the radio. (But can't they do it with sound effects? A dripping tap?)

'It is good to be here!' I glowed.

The water on the flat lake was choppy. Although there had been no wind, or at least not much wind, on the road, down here a cold brisk breeze blew off the lake. Russet gold the reeds. Blue and pewter the lake. Green fields on the far shore.

It must have looked different, on the summer day in 1998, when we first came here and I thought, what a great place for a holiday. Though that, I remember, was a grey overcast day, a not very good Irish summer day.

We did the interview.

We had to keep moving out of the wind. We stood in the shelter of Emma's car, facing the lake. Every so often, a passing vehicle would disturb the recording and I would try to repeat whatever I had been saying when she stopped recording.

It all went well, though, and I felt I had done a good interview, although I could see Emma wince ever so slightly when I said I didn't think 'The Children of Lir' was a very good story. It has a weak storyline. Good folk tales have strong plots. 'The Children of Lir', which grabbed the public imagination soon after it was first translated in about 1850 – just after the Famine – is, I think, a fragment of a real fairy tale – a fairy tale like 'The Twelve Brothers', which you can read in *Grimms' Fairy Tales*, or H.C. Andersen's 'The Wild Swans'. Or else it is a scrappy legend that later evolved into a good story. The scribe messed it up by giving it a Christian ending. It is not in the Irish canon of oral tales. No doubt this has been investigated but I hadn't time to do much research before this interview.

We were finished at about 11.30 and I was in the hospital at 1.

Bo was sitting up in bed. A drip was attached to his arm, a bag to his bladder. He had eaten some lunch.

'I feel tired,' he said.

He had been tired for a year. Sometimes more tired than others. He hated feeling tired, and resisted taking a nap in the afternoons – although he usually did, in the end, and felt better for it. For the past week, since the episode of the tablets, he had been unusually tired.

I sat beside him for just a few minutes, then told the staff nurse I was here and would speak to the doctor whenever possible.

Quite soon – surprisingly soon – a doctor came. He told me Bo's kidneys were not in good condition. He asked me if he had had problems with kidney function.

No. Never.

He told me they were trying hydration.

'We will try it for forty-eight hours or so,' he said.

So. Until Wednesday. Or Thursday at the latest.

'He is old.'

Old? An alarm bell rang in my head. Bo was 82. His sister was 93. His brother lived to be 99, and died one month short of his hundredth birthday. But that was in Sweden, where they have a very good health service. Bo paid what a politician had recently called, sneeringly, 'gold-plated insurance' in order to access a good health service in Ireland, the private health service that had served him well in his cancer treatment and where nobody had mentioned his age. But now, because we had come to the local hospital, and the possibilities for treatment were more limited – he was 'old'. Is that, in fact, a translation of 'dispensable'?

'And with underlying problems – the cancer, diabetes – the outcome can be uncertain.'

Bo didn't have diabetes but I didn't contradict him since it seemed like an unimportant detail. I just stood there, listening, taking it in, feeling increasingly worried.

'If hydration doesn't work, then we will try something else. The worst case scenario is dialysis, or a kidney transplant.'

A kidney transplant. He sensed my shock and spoke gently.

'It is possible that one round of dialysis would get the kidneys functioning again. It does not mean that he would be on dialysis permanently. But first we will try this.'

Okay.

I sat beside Bo and told him, more or less, what the doctor had said. They'll try the drip for a day or two, and see how you get on.

The bag hanging from the side of his bed was filling, slowly.

'It's not a good colour,' the doctor said. 'It should be the colour of straw. Light.'

But it looked normal to me. Normal urine colour. Urine is a pale gold only if you have drunk a lot of water. Most of the time it is a deeper colour. Bo's urine was always a deep colour, and rather strong smelling, and I have the impression that this is how it is, normally, as you get older.

These are the sort of observations you begin to make, in these circumstances. Bo didn't much like talking about his bodily functions. Though he did, of course, to me, a lot, over the past few years. He wouldn't use a chamber pot or anything, but always insisted on going to the bathroom.

Maybe I have a kidney problem too?

The solution dripped steadily from the drip over his bed – which was an ordinary bed, not a hospital bed. It was attached to a machine which set off an alarm if the drip stopped. The alarm rang often, because the drip did not seem to be attached firmly enough to Bo's arm.

The nurse would come and fiddle with the drip and turn off the alarm.

'He keeps pulling it out,' she said.

The contraption looked primitive, to my eyes. I wondered if there were more up-to-date drips, drips that would not detach themselves so easily. I could research that – now – but what good would it do? To Bo? To me?

I sat, Bo dozed, I read my novel.

Two physiotherapists came along.

'We're going to help you get out of bed, and start walking.'

They were pretty young women. Bo smiled and made a joke.

'It's for when you go home. So you'll be well able to move about.'

The curtains were pulled and I moved to the end of the ward. I walked about the hospital.

Loughlinstown is run entirely by the HSE, which makes it unusual in Dublin, where the majority of hospitals are still owned officially by religious orders. On the outside Loughlinstown looks quite attractive – a cluster of long low buildings, with a big bay-window-type door as its main entrance. It nestles in trees, and from its elevated location there is a fine view of a footbridge over the motorway, cushions of trees, and, beyond, the wooded hills of Killiney and Ballybrack. Indeed, on a sunny day – and all the days of the week in question were gloriously bright days – it looks like a delightful hospital. You would imagine that it could be a flagship medical centre for the HSE. Or a perfect site for a private clinic like the Blackrock Clinic.

The entrance area to the main hospital is also quite pleasant – airy, bright, with a little shop to one side, and some brightly-coloured chairs in a waiting area.

Once you leave this hallway, though, everything changes. You are back in another era – the 1950s possibly. Antiques and relics of bygone times are fashionable but nobody wants an old-fashioned hospital.

A very long corridor runs the length of the hospital. Along this corridor are wheelchairs, and other bits and pieces. Handwritten or at least very amateurish posters show arrows for the Eye Clinic. There seem to be dozens of these signs for the Eye Clinic. Bo and I laughed about them, the last time he was in the hospital, trapped for three days after dropping by for an outpatient treatment for constipation (which they treated, very effectively). The corridor is about two hundred yards long, maybe longer. There is one junction, a right-hand turn on to another corridor, that leads to another ward, and to the canteen.

'They have a fantastic canteen,' a nurse in St Vincent's Private Hospital told me. 'There's a brilliant chef. The staff love it. They have to ban patients from it, otherwise they'd be all in there. The food for patients is not great.'

Visitors can use the canteen too. But it is only open for them from 12.30 to 2, and from 5 to 6. For the rest of the time there are no facilities for refreshments apart from vending machines full of crisps and chocolate. There is a vending machine for coffee but it was broken for a few days during this week.

At the end of the long corridor is the ward specialising in geriatric care. You open a door and pass a toilet. Sometimes the public hospitals have a serious shortage of toilets and bathrooms. I remember my mother, a patient in St Vincent's University Hospital – that is, the public part – a dying patient, was distressed because they never gave her a shower or washed her hair. She was there for weeks, and had to use a dry shampoo to make her hair look reasonably presentable. (Do you care about your hair when you are very ill? Yes. You do. She did.)

Next there is a desk – the nurses' station – and a room marked 'Staff Only'.

Then a series of wards – maybe four – with six beds to each ward. The beds are very close together. There is space for one chair beside each bed, no more. There is a sense of clutter everywhere – it is cluttered because there are too many people in a small space. It is completely different from the calm, spacious, clinical emptiness of the room Bo had in Vincent's Private, rooms with big windows looking out over the Dublin mountains or the golf club, rooms with chairs for visitors, with their own bathrooms. All that.

I remember what it was like in the 1950s. I was in Harcourt Street Children's Hospital for about ten days, with an ear abscess, and 'getting my tonsils out', as almost everyone did then. My bed was in the corner of a big ward, with perhaps twelve beds in it. My mother was allowed to visit for one hour a day. This was before I could read and I was very bored. After the operation, I was in great pain for days, maybe weeks – I could only eat jelly or ice cream. But the ward was spacious and airy, with high ceilings, and plenty of room between beds. That's how I remember it. Of course, I was five or six – everything looked big.

In the ward that Bo was in you could reach out and touch the patient in the bed next to you. Almost. Is this healthy?

In the bed to the right of Bo was a big red-faced man. Bob? Some such name. On this day, the first day, Bob was having some trouble with his breathing, and had an oxygen mask over his face most of the time. A blessing, although we didn't know that yet. In the bed opposite was a small neat man called Pat. Pat was up and about. He was very tidily dressed, in black pants, neatly belted, and a white shirt.

When I got back, the physiotherapists were finished with Bo. He was sitting on the chair by the bed but asked to be put back in. He felt tired. They helped him back – with great difficulty. Bo, who on Sunday could walk downstairs, sit at the kitchen table, sit in his big red chair in the living room and watch *Downton Abbey*, on Tuesday could not get out of a chair and get into bed.

Why didn't we ask questions about this? Had he broken a bone? Had he been X-rayed? I will find the answers to these questions two years later, in a report I commissioned from an expert consultant in England, who examined the medical files. The answer is yes, there was a small fracture, and no, apparently he was not X-rayed.

I asked Bo if he would like to read *Bombi Bitt och Jag*, the little white first edition that was lying on his locker. He shook his head. The big black Parkinson history lay like a sombre cliff beside *Bombi Bitt*. My stomach tightened when I looked at it. This was the first time in his life that Bo was unable to read. Unwilling to read. Maybe not the first time. There have been hours when he has recovered from operations, when he was emerging from anaesthetic. He could not read then. But he

118

always recovered very quickly, in hardly any time at all, usually. And if he was awake at all, he always wanted to read.

'Bo is very resilient,' I would say, triumphantly, when people asked. And it was true.

But now he hadn't had an operation. He wasn't very ill. It's nothing serious. They'll hydrate him, he'll be out in a day or so.

The drip wasn't attached to him now. They'd disconnected it while they were pulling him about for the physiotherapy. I mentioned this to the nurse and she said she'd connect it but she didn't, for a while.

The atmosphere in this ward: relaxed, weary, messy.

I hadn't had anything to eat since about 7 a.m., so I went to check out the canteen, which has such a good reputation, the shining light of Loughlinstown. It was closed. I tried the coffee vending machine. It took my coins but no coffee emerged. I could have asked someone about coffee – the man who looked like a security man, the woman in the sweetshop – but I didn't.

That's the trouble with me. I don't ask. I don't complain enough, directly enough, to the right people. I don't react quickly enough. And now I didn't know how urgent the situation was. I didn't realise that time was running out.

I sat with Bo. He was half-asleep, half-awake. I talked a little, he talked. His voice had become a little weaker, but it was still Bo's voice, rich, round, warm, ironic, Swedish. I gave him drinks of water. The drip had been reattached. The alarm bell went off, when he lay on the tube, when it loosened in his hand, already bruised cruelly. The bag with the liquid seemed to be too low over the bed – it looked to me as if gravity could do more to help the flow, if it were positioned higher. How amateurish it looks! And yet I didn't really know, couldn't remember enough to compare it to other bags I had seen. All I could remember was the room in Vincent's Private, its professional clean clinical look, the sense of security you had there, partly engendered by the look of the place. Of course, people are very sick, people die, in such hospitals, too, but you know that the best medicine, the best equipment, the best medical staff, are available. You feel as safe as is humanly possible. Here in Loughlinstown I felt the opposite. I sensed danger. They don't have sodium that can be taken orally. They don't have this and they don't have that – later a nurse will rather crossly tell me that they don't have containers for dentures, could I bring some in myself. And all too soon I will find out that they don't have other crucial life-saving equipment.

Meanwhile, a phone call.

It's Emma. From the radio. 'Children of Lir' Emma.

I have missed a few calls from her.

She doesn't know how to tell me this, she says. But the computer card on which she recorded my interview was corrupt. She can't retrieve the recording.

The morning – the drive to Lough Derravaragh, the golden trees, the bleak choppy waters of the lake, all my good ideas about 'The Children of Lir' – gone. Three hours when I could have been here with Bo.

'They've been trying but they can't get it.'

'These things happen.'

'I could do it again if you can come to Lough Derravaragh again sometime this week.'

'No, I wouldn't be able to do that.'

She didn't offer to redo the interview in the studio, which surprised me, but I didn't suggest it. I didn't want to.

'I'll cancel it.'

'It's okay, Emma. These things happen. Goodbye.'

I just wanted her off the phone. I wanted to get back to Bo. Now our life was the hospital ward. The outside world was irrelevant.

Pat came over and straightened Bo's slippers, which were on the floor at the end of the bed. He went to the window at the end of the ward and pulled back the curtains. A nurse, small, bright, young, commended him.

'You're always helping me, Pat!' she said.

She came and talked to me and Bo. She's a student nurse, a

warm and kind person, a wonderful nurse. The young student nurses, the student doctors, were among the most considerate people, the most caring people, in this hospital. I told her Bo's drip didn't seem to be working properly. She looked at it and agreed.

'I'm not allowed to do anything with it,' she said, regretfully. 'I'll ask the nurse.'

But nobody came.

I went home at about half past five, to touch base at the house, and to get something to eat. By now I had texted our sons to let them know that Bo was in hospital, and I'd texted Marja, Bo's daughter. I telephoned my next-door neighbour, Gari, who had left two or three messages on the answering machine. I asked her for advice on how to move Bo to another hospital. She suggested that I telephone the Blackrock Clinic and ask them. I decided that I would work on this problem on Wednesday. She also thought that I should find out where the consultant Bo had been assigned to had his private practice.

'They usually have clinics in Blackrock and Vincent's as well as there.' This seemed like a good idea.

Back in the hospital, the drip had been inserted again and seemed to be functioning. The monitoring machine had been switched off, however, so the nurses would not know when the drip slipped out. They would no longer be annoyed by the alarm.

Marja and Ragnar came to see Bo, and so did Olaf and Nadezhda. Bo was very glad to see them, and talked cheerfully enough, if weakly. It was a pleasant evening. Tuesday.

DAY 60

Copenhagen

I was all dressed up in my off-white outfit, my favourite summer clothes: skirt, blouse, straw-coloured espadrilles. A straw basket instead of a handbag. In the basket, hairbrush, purse, passport. A few traveller's cheques.

I had checked in all my luggage. An enormous suitcase. My portable typewriter in its neat grey case. Portable, it nevertheless weighed six or seven kilos. The woman on the check-in desk had advised me to stow it. There seemed to be no limit to the amount of luggage you could check in.

I chatted to a couple on the plane, on their way back from a holiday in Ireland. They told me they found the white bread people in Ireland ate unbelievable. The sliced pans. We would never eat such bread. Maybe for breakfast. It does not fill you up.

The woman had curly fair hair, a kind of hair I would forevermore associate with Danish women. Swedes and Finns tend to have the straight flaxen styles, Danes have the curls.

The plane left Dublin at three in the afternoon and arrived in Copenhagen at nine o'clock. In those days, the Aer Lingus flight to Copenhagen, gateway to Scandinavia, stopped over at Manchester for an hour, to let passengers on and off. The hour stretched to an hour and a half.

Passport control. Customs.

The luggage belt.

Exactly the same then as now. The bags coming round and

round. People waiting anxiously, hoping to spot theirs as it came through the gap. Diving on it when it passed them. It's like the game children play in streams – setting a paper boat afloat and catching it when it comes bobbing through under the bridge.

My big brown case didn't come bobbing through, nor did my little typewriter case.

I waited and waited.There were no notices then – that was a difference. You didn't get a message saying 'Dublin first bag, Dublin last bag' as you do now. When everyone was gone and there were no bags left I began to panic, and to wonder what I was supposed to do next. I was not an experienced traveller. Far from it.

Somehow I found an official; I filled in a form. My address in Copenhagen. There was a phone number to ring.

Then I was on a bus, which brought me to Central Station. Hovedbanegård. My reading of *Babette* meant I could figure out some of the signs. Information I could have figured anyway. I couldn't speak a word of Danish or understand anything people were saying, but I managed to get a ticket to Albertslund. Where I would live. The Kollegium. Vognporten 14.

It's a twenty-minute train journey from Hovedbanegård to Albertslund. In the dark, train journeys seem much longer.

Albertslund Station is a suburban station, still very new in 1978. At eleven o'clock at night it was almost deserted. There was nobody in the ticket office, and the shutters on the kiosk were closed. When you alighted from the train you had to go through a tunnel, which branched – of course – in two directions. I had no idea where the Kollegium was. Somehow it had not occurred to me that I was lacking this knowledge until I got out of the train. There were many questions that I should have asked, before I found myself alone on a platform in a suburb of Copenhagen in the middle of the night.

A woman dressed in a hijab came down the tunnel steps, a small boy holding her hand. Women with children always look safe. They're probably not going to stab you if you ask them a question.

'Do you speak English?'

'*Nej, nej,*' the woman shook her head vigorously.

'Danmarks Internationale Kollegium?' I persisted.

The woman shook her head. Then the little boy said something to her. She smiled and pointed. Since we were underground this was not as useful as it could have been, but she indicated left and then left again.

'Thank you,' I knew the word in Danish for thanks but felt too shy to say it.

The directions were correct. I emerged on to a road that was called Vognporten. To my left, just above the railway track, was a big building belching out smoke – a factory? The heating plant for Albertslund, I found out later. A signpost pointed to DIK, Danmarks Internationale Kollegium. I could see it, at the end of the road – a collection of long low buildings, glowing with a gentle, friendly orange light, in the blackness, like ships on a calm dark sea.

My heart lifted.

The summer air was warm and soft on the skin and my white skirt felt light and fleet as wings, as, reinvigorated, I walked towards my destination, the glowing ships in the welcoming harbour.

Not quite.

An Arctic explorer would have been better prepared. Åmundson wouldn't have reached the North Pole if he had been one tenth as careless as I was.

Because only when I reached the first of the long white houses did I realise that I would have to get a key, get a room number.

Check in.

Checking in was something I had never done before in my life.

When I went on holidays I stayed with aunties in the country. You didn't have to check in with them – they never went anywhere; they would be at home no matter when you arrived. My holidays abroad had been working holidays: once in a small hotel on the Isle of Wight, once in a cafe on one of the Frisian islands. (Islands patterned my travelling life, by accident rather than by design.) The owners of those places were like the aunts. They were always at home. They were at home in houses that had a front door, and a knocker or a bell.

There was nothing like that in evidence here.

I walked along the grass by the side of one of the long buildings. There were lights in windows, and one room was a kitchen, all lit up. I peered through the big window. It looked very cosy inside, warmly coloured, orange and oak. But empty.

It was getting later and later. Would I have to sleep on the grass, under a tree? Clad in nothing but my light cotton blouse and skirt?

I saw a young man walking along the path towards one of the buildings. I ran up to him.

'Do you speak English?'

'Yes.'

He was small and thin with ragged hair like straw and a pasty complexion. But his eyes were big and soft.

I explained the situation.

He looked worried.

'Herr Rasmussen is not here now.' He glanced at his watch and shrugged. 'He'll be here tomorrow at nine o'clock.'

'Who is he?'

'The man who gives out the keys.' He showed me the building where Herr Rasmussen's office was, close to the entrance to the harbour of residences. It was locked and dark.

'Thank you.'

'Goodnight.'

He headed off, to his room, leaving me standing there, outside the office that would open at nine o'clock in the morning.

I watched his retreating back as if it was my last hope.

It had not occurred to me to ask him if there was a hotel in

Albertslund. It didn't look like the kind of place where there would be an hotel, as far as I could see. In fact, at this hour, it looked as if every inhabitant of Albertslund was fast asleep in bed. It had not occurred to me to ask if there was somewhere I could sleep in the Kollegium. There was – there were sofas in the living room. But why would he allow a stranger in, to sleep there? Even a female stranger in a white cotton blouse and skirt, who looked harmless.

I got the train back to Hovedbanegård. The trains run late, in Copenhagen.

And at the station, an information office was still open, although it was almost midnight. A big brisk woman with the dry blond hair many older woman had gave me the names of some nearby hotels. She picked the cheapest, on Absalon Gade, which was just around the corner. Going beyond the call of duty she phoned the hotel and made a reservation.

And still I had to find the hotel. It was small and seedy, not like a hotel at all. The lobby was a tiny hallway, the receptionist a fat middle-aged man, who didn't look as if he had washed that day. My room was the size of a matchbox, beige coloured, grubby – this was a kind of hotel that perhaps does not exist any more, a cheap, shabby hotel by a railway station, just across from the huge five stars, the Scandic and the Radisson and the SAS. Through my window I could see the big SAS sign glowing in the night. But I was in a room; I could lock the door. Tomorrow was Saturday, but Herr Rasmussen would be in his office from nine. I would start again.

How lucky that I had not arrived on Saturday night!

Breakfast: a coffee (not bad – the coffee in Denmark is always good) and a soft white roll in a plastic wrapper. One pat of butter and one plastic capsule of jam. The dining room was a tiny drab anteroom to the hall. It was also beige, everything was beige and drab – the antithesis of everything I had expected Denmark to be – or expected a hotel to be.

The other guests seemed to be old men, who looked at me

inquisitively. I was curious too. Who were they? Who stayed in a place like this?

I had washed – there was a towel and a tiny pat of hard nasty-smelling soap in the bathroom (special tiny pats of soap must be specially made for these places … you never get them anywhere else). I had some make-up in the straw basket, but no toothpaste or deodorant or anything of that kind. Already I felt sticky and sweaty. There were dark stains under the arms of the blouse and a fine patina of dust covered all the expanse of creamy cloth, which yesterday was fresh and new.

On Nørrebrogade, though, the sun was shining.

I checked out, parting nervously with a lot of money – my store of kroner, acquired in the AIB bank on Grafton Street, was diminishing much too fast. Another ticket to Albertslund. The journey seemed shorter, in daylight, but I was not ready to enjoy the view of Copenhagen's suburbs, or the exotic placenames. Dybbølsbro. Lyngby. Hvidovre. The pleasure of the foreign names would wait for another day.

What a relief to find Herr Rasmussen in place, sitting at his desk. A white-haired man, with a narrow scholarly-looking face, glasses.

He consulted a list.

I worried that my name would not be on it. That my reservation would not have been received. I would always worry about this, for my entire life, checking in at airports, at hotels. I would always worry that I had made some mistake. He read down the list. A minute. At least it was still daylight. At least the sun was shining. Two minutes.

He smiled and handed me a key.

He walked with me to my room, in Block Two, on the ground floor.

He showed me around. My post box in his office area. The communal kitchen in Block Two. The television room. My own room.

Small. Modern. Stylish. Clean as a whistle.

As Danish as Danish could be.

A bed, a wooden desk with a red trim, a grey armchair. Bookshelves. My own bathroom. A sliding door, a French window, opening on to the narrow lawn. A small willow tree outside.

I lay on the bed, for a moment, relieved to have a bed, a room, a door key. My rent I had paid a month in advance. In September, my scholarship money would start coming in. The scholarship was £250 pounds a month – 2,500 kroner. The rent was £80. I didn't know if I would have enough to live on. But in my straw basket I had enough money to live for a month.

There was the problem of the suitcase. No clothes apart from those on my back. And – another surprise – the room contained no bed linen, no towels. No blanket. It was basically furnished, and in the communal kitchen all necessary cooking utensils and crockery and so on were provided. But I had to get a sheet and some sort of bed cover, and a towel. Or two?

In Albertslund Centrum was an Irma supermarket, a bakery, a hardware store, and a drapery of kinds. Also a library and a cinema. I bought a thin duvet, a sheet and a towel in the drapery. Shopped for food in the Irma.

The food thrilled me. It was quite different from what I was used to. Rye bread. Liver pâté. Marinated herrings. Real coffee. Going around the supermarket was an adventure.

The first days in a new place are the most memorable. In the case of Copenhagen, they were memorable because they were difficult, a hassle. Never again would I arrive in a new country so unprepared, so ignorant of how things worked. Nobody – my parents, Bo, Oliver – had asked the question: where will you go when you land in Copenhagen at nine o'clock on Friday night? My parents had no clue about foreign countries. They never travelled abroad. Denmark might as well be the moon as far as they were concerned. Bo I had not seen for some weeks prior to my departure. He had gone to Kerry, as he always did, around the start of July, and he wasn't even aware of the details of my travel plans – otherwise the question might have been asked. Oliver had recent experience of travelling as a student. But on his first arrival in Ireland he had stayed with a family. Families are like aunties; always at home, early or late, when they're expecting a guest. On his subsequent arrivals, he had friends to fall back on – me and my family in the first instance. So maybe it hadn't occurred to him to ask the question: what happens when you arrive?

I was more like Robinson Crusoe, that first night, than like any Arctic explorer. A castaway, adrift in the dark of Copenhagen. And I was still like him, two and three days later, gathering supplies and utensils, still waiting for my suitcase to arrive from the airport.

The year in Copenhagen was full of adventure. I learned to speak Danish fluently. I wrote a good part of my thesis, I attended classes in the Folklore Institute, I made many friends. It was one of the best years of my life. But that is all another story.

Everything I reported back to Bo, in a regular correspondence, letters two or three times a week, back and forth. The correspondence was interrupted for a few months by the postmen's strike in Ireland, during which contact was almost impossible. Bo still had no phone in his flat. I had access to the coin box in the hall in Albertslund. Once or twice Bo called, from a coin box or from his office. Someone would answer the phone, then come and knock on my door.

Oliver wrote a few times but the correspondence soon fizzled out. My heart was not in it and neither was his.

Finally, he wrote to protest about a short story I published. The story was fictional, but had been inspired by an episode, not a pleasant one, in our relationship. 'Do not use me in your productions,' Oliver wrote, furiously.

I was furious too. The characters in my story bore no resemblance to us. Only Oliver and I would have recognised that the episode was based on a real event. While I know very well that nobody appreciates finding themselves or their actions depicted in fiction, even if they are presented in a good light, this now seems to me a classic male attempt at censorship and control.

But what annoyed me most was the use of the word 'productions'. Not story, work, fiction.

I never wrote to him again.

Trying to escape

On Wednesday morning, I rang the hospital. Bo was all right, according to the nurse. I asked to speak to the consultant under whose care Bo had been placed. The telephonist said she would connect me. But the person I put through to was not the consultant but a member of his team. I told her I was interested in getting Bo transferred to a private room or to a private hospital. She was sympathetic and said she would see me when I came in, just to ask for her.

I set to work, my goal being to have Bo moved to a good hospital. That was my priority for Wednesday. I wanted to get him away from the antique-looking drip, from the crowded ward, and into a hospital where he would have comfort and dignity. I still didn't realise that the main difference between the private hospital and this HSE institution was that the medical care in the former would be much superior; I still didn't realise that this HSE hospital could lack more than stylishness and comfort. I was still in ordinary time, concerned with aesthetics, not that they are unimportant.

First I telephoned the clinic in which Bo had received his cancer treatment in Vincent's Private. I spoke to one of the medical secretaries.

'He needs a nephrologist,' she said. 'We don't have many. We have one or two here.'

'So what should I do?'

'You need to ask one of them to take Bo as a patient.'

'Thank you.'

I didn't phone one of the nephrologists. Who were they? How could I telephone complete strangers and ask them to take Bo out of Loughlinstown and into St Vincent's Private? Instead I decided to ring the urologist who used to treat Bo in the Private Outpatients' Clinic attached to Loughlinstown and in the Blackrock Clinic. Surely this was a urological problem to some extent? Anyway he is someone we knew and liked. But when I phoned his clinic, an answering service told me he would be away until 24 November. This was Wednesday 6 November. (Gustav Adolf's Dag – if we had gone to Uppsala, as usual, none of this would be happening.) I then telephoned the GP, who was not available but who would phone me back. Finally I tried to trace the consultant. I hoped he would have a private clinic somewhere. The website for Loughlinstown supplies no information about its consultants, about its staff. I was beginning to wonder if this consultant was actually in situ in the hospital. Perhaps he was represented by his team? I checked the lists of consultants in Blackrock, Vincent's, and the Beacon. There was no reference on any of the lists to this particular consultant. I wondered if he actually existed.

Two hours on the net and phone got me precisely nowhere.

I went to the hospital.

The doctor that I had spoken to on the phone earlier saw me. She was very reassuring.

'Bo is responding slowly to the hydration,' she said. 'A bit slower than we anticipated, but it will work in time.'

Wednesday lunchtime. It will work.

I pointed out that the drip was actually not functioning as we spoke (and I wondered if it had functioned at all, during the night, when I was not there. The bag of urine was half empty.).

'I'll put it in myself,' she said.

She put it in deftly, more neatly than it had been inserted before, and I was impressed by her skill and kindness.

I pointed out that Bo's stomach was swollen, but she touched it and seemed unconcerned.

She explained that there were no private rooms in Loughlinstown, and that patients couldn't be transferred to another hospital just to get a private room.

I explained, tactfully, that we were very happy with everything – everyone was good and the care excellent (which was a barefaced lie, but I thought it diplomatic to be complimentary). But it was not the right environment for Bo. He needed quiet. And if he had to stay in for a while he would have a lot of visitors. There's nowhere for visitors to be, in this ward.

'Believe me, I know where you're coming from,' she said. 'If it were my parent I'd put them in the car and drive them to the Blackrock Clinic or the Beacon, I wouldn't call an ambulance. But he'll be out soon probably.'

I sat by the bed.

Bob, in the bed next to Bo's, had had his nebuliser removed. This enabled him to shout abuse at the nurses as they went about their work.

'You fucking bitch, come and help me! Where are the cunts?'

He had a very loud voice and a violently angry face, but he seemed to be secured in his bed in some way. At least he couldn't get up to attack anyone. The staff were stoically oblivious to the abusive remarks he directed at them, which flowed out in a torrent whenever he was not wearing his nebuliser.

'Fucking bastard! I'll slit your throat!'

Possibly he was an Alzheimer's case? One of those whose personality changes under the influence of the disease, who are transformed into monsters by it? Nobody explained. The other patients, and visitors, had to listen to his stream of invective.

Pat, in his black pants and white shirt, came over and

straightened Bo's slippers at the end of the bed. I smiled at him, and nodded my thanks.

In the afternoon, the GP phoned the hospital to find out how Bo was, and later he phoned me on my mobile. I went out on to the dark corridor to take the call. I asked him if he could help me to get Bo transferred to Vincent's Private.

He said I would have to talk to the consultant in Loughlinstown and get him to agree to a transfer. Then I would have to get a consultant in Vincent's to agree to take Bo.

At that moment, I thought: If Bo dies in Loughlinstown I will never forgive these doctors.

But I didn't say it. Not out of consideration for his feelings, but because then, on Wednesday, the prospect that Bo might die still seemed so remote as to be unthinkable.

On Wednesday night, Olaf came out to visit, alone. He and I sat with Bo. Bo had now been re-bedded in a proper hospital bed, the kind that can be raised, so he was more comfortable. The drip did not seem to be functioning properly, although it was inserted.

'It's working,' Olaf said.

It was dripping but very, very, very slowly, a tiny little drip about once every thirty seconds. Had it moved faster, earlier? Was there a reason for this slowdown? The bag of urine seemed not to have increased at all since morning.

Bo, half sitting up, was hallucinatory, for the first and only time.

He talked, a lot.

He believed he was sitting in the car. He talked about secondary roads and main roads, we should take this road, and that road. I engaged in the conversation. He believed we were in the car, driving around the Fanad peninsula in Donegal, as we had been doing just a week earlier. He was remembering the little roads of Fanad – a criss-crossing network, passing lakes and humpbacked hills, mountains and sea, farms and churches and islands, from Fanad lighthouse down to Kerrykeel and Magherawarden.

We drove the roads again, in the hospital ward.

'Emmet,' he said.

'Robert Emmet?' asked Olaf.

'I have a nephew named Emmet, do I not?' Bo asked.

'Yes, you do.'

We both laughed. Olaf was disturbed, more disturbed than I was, by Bo's ramblings. It didn't upset me since I found it easy to enter into the spirit of it, as if I were walking or talking in Bo's dream. And it passed quickly, as I knew it would. Bo slept. A hospital worker, wearing a uniform like a garda, came around and rang a bell and asked us to leave.

Olaf took the 145 back to his apartment in town, and I went home.

The Thousandth Day

We continued to meet in secret, in Bo's apartment, from September 1979 until May 1982 – two and a half years.

The secret became more widely known. In May 1981, for instance, we celebrated Bo's fiftieth birthday with a party in the flat to which two of his colleagues and their wives, as well as Bo's daughter, Marja, were invited. My family too knew of the relationship. I was living at home again, which I found difficult, but Bo advised against moving out. We were to be married as soon as I finished my PhD. What was the point? I spent weekends, at least one night a week, at his apartment, anyway.

As soon as I returned from Denmark I got a job on the Urban Folklore Project, collecting folklore in Dublin. This was a dream job, independent, interesting. It involved meeting all kinds of people, interviewing them, recording them, transcribing the recordings.

Although I was now working in my field, it was in a position that was both menial, in the sense that it was badly paid, and anomalous. A big youth employment scheme – eighteen people were working on it, some with qualifications in the subject, some not. Nobody was going to ask questions about my right to such a job, which would last for eighteen months. The question of a career in folklore, the subject I was working on for my PhD, and in which I was passionately interested and now, after a year of intensive study in Copenhagen about which I was very knowledgeable, was uppermost in my mind. Bo preferred to push it under the carpet. We did not discuss how it would be possible for me to work in this field. In Dublin, in Ireland, there was only one place in which the subject could be pursued professionally, namely UCD, where he was head of department. I persisted in believing that since this was the case, since there was only one possible place of employment for someone with my qualifications, I was entitled to apply for any job that came up. Jobs didn't come up very often, needless to say, and there would be several applicants for anything that did arise. That I would be viewed with resentment and suspicion if I happened to get one of these jobs did not bother me much. Bo seemed not overly concerned about it either. The problem was in any event hypothetical.

The 1980s was a decade of recession and unemployment. Many young people emigrated. Recruitment to the public service and the universities was limited. 'Embargo' was a word in common parlance. Embargo on recruitment, embargo on promotion. 'Frozen' was the adjective increasingly used in relation to positions. A job could be advertised and filled – and then frozen: that is, not filled. Or advertised, and frozen just before candidates were interviewed. This happened in connection with a few university positions of which I was aware, not in my field.

Curiously, the National Library advertised for Assistant Keepers Grade Two in January 1981. I had finally handed in my doctorate, which had taken five years to complete – given that I was working full time for four of those years, and learning a new language and participating full time in university courses for one of them, it was not a very long time, but it seemed long. Five years during which my relationship with Oliver had ended, my relationship with Bo had started and continued, during which I had had three different jobs and one year abroad. The years of my twenties. I was twenty-two when I started my PhD and twenty-seven when I handed it in for assessment.

I, who had vowed never to return to the National Library, applied. There was little else to apply for; nothing, in fact. Not having an income was an impossible situation. I didn't consider the dole. Nobody in my family knew anything about it. It wasn't that we were prejudiced against it, particularly. It was simply terra incognita to us. We were the sort of working-class people who always worked, and, as somebody once pointed out to me, in some bewilderment, I seemed to 'like working' and to get jobs easily. From the moment I finished the BA, in September 1974, until January 1982, I had never been without some sort of regular income – from jobs, scholarships, tutoring. Something. I felt at a complete loss when I realised that at the end of the week beginning 1 January, there would be no money at all coming in.

This was a class preoccupation, the desperate need for paid employment. Working class. My more bourgeois friends had no difficulty enduring periods of unemployment – they had a certain sense of entitlement, and, I think, a sense of security. They could say things that sounded quite outlandish, such as, 'Well, the only thing I know how to do is write.' Or 'paint'. They might as well have been saying, 'The only thing I know how to do is play marbles.' I laughed when I heard some of these proclamations, from aspiring artists or academics who really believed that they were speaking from a position of necessity, who genuinely believed that they 'could not' work in an office, or a school, not to mention a factory, when it was abundantly clear that they spoke from a position of choice. Only people with money somewhere in their background could afford the luxury of such firm self-belief, such glorious ambitions to live lives that did not, for a start, oblige them to get up early in the morning and clock in. 'I don't do mornings!' I had heard one of those people say. 'I can't do a job that involves getting dressed every morning.'

Did they really believe that everyone who had a job felt born to get up early in the morning, wash and dress, catch a bus, and work all day in an office or a shop or a field until 5.30 or 6? Did they really believe that all those people had chosen to do that, rather than 'not do mornings' and write a great book?

It wasn't a choice open to me. There was no money to shore me up while I 'found myself' – accepting the scholarship to Denmark was as wild and free and reckless as I was ever going to get. I belonged to the ranks of those who have to earn their living. So I applied to the library and, to my surprise – and to that of many people – was offered the post again.

In 1978 I had left the library. And now in April 1982, almost four years later, I was back. It was a relief to get a job, and, in 1982, something of a miracle. With very mixed feelings I took up the position.

Some changes had occurred. There were a few new staff members. The previous director had taken another job, as head of one of the university libraries, and been replaced. I sat in a different room, a much nicer room, than the one I had been in previously. The work of checking catalogues continued, but there seemed to be a lot less of it. The atmosphere was lighter, more optimistic, more cheerful.

The National Library had begun its march out of the nineteenth century and into modernity. It was a much happier and more stimulating environment than it had been in the 1970s.

A few weeks after I started working in the library, I was conferred with my doctorate. Bo joined me and my family for a celebration dinner, in a restaurant that was popular just then: a cosy bistro on Pleasant Street, off Camden Street – the area that would soon be called Portobello, and become very fashionable, but was still in transit from slummy to trendy.

Now there was no reason to postpone the marriage further. Looking at the little houses on Pleasant Street, and Synge Street, some of which were rundown and some of which were being newly gentrified, with geraniums on the windowsills, the thought crossed my mind that I would like to live in a place like this.

Love can go smoothly, or it can, as in fairy tales, involve a series of tests.

I had been tested several times already, more than most, perhaps. There was the issue of Bo's age – I had to overcome my own and my family's and the wider community's prejudices and just do what I wanted to do. There was the Oliver hurdle which I had stumbled over ingloriously rather than tackling with noble dignity. There was the PhD – Bo was definite that no marriage could occur until the doctorate was finished. At first I was fully in agreement with him, but as time, and the PhD, dragged on, I wondered if it was such a good idea to wait. I was determined to finish it – the idea of not finishing never crossed my mind. But I believed I could be married and finishing a PhD at the same time; that I could find a new supervisor, and that indeed that might have been preferable.

But now that hurdle was crossed. I was a doctor. My photograph appeared in the newspapers, smiling at the camera in my red gown and black cap, clutching my rolled-up scroll, my PhD.

In the library, everyone congratulated me. But more than one decided they should let me know that my achievement was not worth much. They told anecdotes about jobs for junior office workers. Half the applicants had PhDs. The folly of it all!

So many doctorates out there! Nevertheless, there was only one other doctor on the staff of the entire library, but I accepted these anecdotes as the truth. PhDs were two a penny. I had achieved nothing special. On the contrary, some of these men in the library, who had BAs, were telling me I was a bit of a fool for having worked so hard for what was essentially a worthless piece of paper.

In fact, although I didn't think to check the statistics, I belonged to a tiny minority. There was a reason for the photos in the national newspapers. Very few women, especially women aged twenty-eight, were awarded with the degree of doctor in Ireland in 1982. Relatively few ever are, in this country. To finish a PhD is a considerable achievement, and only those who are doctors know how much work is involved. In my case, I had learnt to read several languages, explored the cultures of most of the countries in northern Europe, and read widely in the fields of folklore and ethnology, in order to write my thesis.

Now it was done. I had the passport to marriage to Bo, and a full-time, well-paid job in the library, albeit the same job I had had when I was starting the PhD.

But there were more hurdles to cross.

First, Bo became depressed.

The prospect of marriage wasn't the reason for the depression, or the ostensible reason, although that the attack came around the time I finished the doctorate could hardly have been entirely coincidental. Now, what had been almost a fantasy, a vague prospect on the distant horizon, was realised. Soon – there were more barriers than either of us realised – we could be married.

Marriage is a stressful life event. On the Holmes and Rahe scale of stressful events, it comes somewhere in the top ten. Losing a spouse is number one, followed by divorce and separation. Losing a job, going to prison. But marriage is there, among all these events involving loss, at about seven or eight. It's the only positive event that causes so much stress. I'm not sure why exactly. Because it involves loss of freedom? Because it is such a serious commitment? The mechanics of big weddings clearly create a lot of – needless – stress for some people, but the big fat wedding, which we were definitely not planning to have, is not 'marriage', as such.

What appeared to precipitate the distress was something quite different. Bo was invited to do a lecture tour in Scandinavia – Norway, Sweden, Finland. He would visit six or seven universities and lecture on a topic of his choice. This invitation had come in the late autumn and the tour was to take place in the summer term, April or May.

He accepted the invitation, which was an honour, and began to work on papers.

The easy, and obvious, and expected, way to handle a lecture tour of that kind is to write one lecture and deliver a version of it in all the venues. Bo's predecessor, Séamus Delargy, wrote 'The Gaelic Storyteller' – one of very few scholarly articles he ever wrote, in fact, since he was an activist and administrator rather than a researcher – and gave the lecture wherever he went. It was, and remained for half a century, one of the definitive works on storytelling in Ireland. Bo would have been expected to do something similar – a survey work, impressions of the state of the art of storytelling in particular and oral tradition in general in Ireland today.

But he had a difficulty.

Bo was a scholar of a particular bent: he was a comparative philologist and folklorist. He loved literature, languages and learning, and was outstandingly knowledgeable in the fields of oral literature in Ireland, Iceland and Scandinavia, and was well versed in history and anthropology in general. He had been educated in an empirical school and distrusted theory and speculation. 'In scholarship there are no shortcuts.' His preferred, his established, method was to study in minute detail specific texts, from oral tradition and literature, to chart their history, and to comment on their context and meaning. Any theory he had was strictly evidence-based and he disliked generalisations. The school of research in which he had been trained was scientific in its methods.

But folkloristics had changed since Bo's day, in Uppsala and Iceland in the 1950s. One of the reasons he had left Sweden was that standards had dropped so drastically, as he saw it. Folklore had become ethnology – the student revolution of 1968 had had dramatic consequences for the study of folklore in Sweden and much of Scandinavia. 'We want no old books!' had been the slogan on a placard in a demonstration against the traditional study of literature on Carolinabacken, the hill on which the great library of Uppsala sits. Students didn't want to study the classical texts in literature, and in folklore they no longer wanted to learn about the old stories and legends, the medieval sources. They didn't want to learn languages, old or, it seemed, new (apart from English).

In Denmark, I had encountered the new ways. The professor in Copenhagen had advised me to stop writing my thesis on the Chaucerian folk tale, and select a more up-to date topic. 'Nobody has written a historical–geographical monograph in the past thirty years in Denmark,' he said. He himself, Bengt Holbeck, was writing a mammoth work on the meaning of fairy tales – a book which was both scholarly and evidence-based, and imaginative and theoretical. I would have liked to work on something similar. I had suggested to Bo that I switch and study the storytelling of women in Ireland, a topic which had not been investigated at all at that point in time, but he had persuaded me not to change.

In Copenhagen, students were writing dissertations on the celebration of May Day in contemporary Denmark, on gardening as a hobby in North Zealand, on the work practices and customs of chimney sweeps in Copenhagen.

Since coming to Ireland in 1972, Bo had seldom gone to an international conference. He visited Iceland occasionally, where he lectured on topics related to Icelandic literature and folklore, and he liked to attend events on the Faroes, and on Shetland and Orkney. Otherwise he focussed exclusively on Ireland. He considered conferences a waste of time, and in any case he was always extremely busy in UCD, running a department and an archive, editing an annual journal, *Béaloideas*, which he transformed from being a journal of folklore texts to a research journal that was gradually gaining an international reputation. In his free time he collected folklore in Kerry and spent a great deal of time transcribing stories he had recorded from Micheál Ó Gaoithín and Bab Feirtéar. He also worked consistently on a huge edition of the stories of Peig Sayers.

While it is true that he was very busy, took his duties very seriously, and saw the collecting, editing, surveying and analysis of Irish folklore as the most important work in the world, and did not have much time for anything else, it is possible that he preferred to avoid the international folkloristic scene. He was regarded as old-fashioned in his approach. His detailed focus on individual texts, the historic dissemination patterns, was considered dull, and his refusal to engage with modern theory marginalised him in a world where folklore research was increasingly driven by theory – Marxism, structuralism, formalism, feminism. Bo was a liberal humanist, but, like most liberal humanists, he did not categorise himself. (They are like writers of literary fiction in this way. We don't regard literary fiction as a 'genre', but tend to believe it is the only fiction. This attitude is increasingly challenged by writers in 'genre' fiction – quite rightly, I believe.) Liberal humanism still held sway in literary studies in Ireland, but even here was about to be replaced by more consciously theoretical approaches.

Bo realised that he was expected to provide some general insight into Irish folklore and Irish folklore studies, but he rejected any notion of writing a journalistic type of lecture – which is what 'The Gaelic Storyteller', for instance, is – a series of informed impressions. It wasn't in his nature to write such things, although in conversation it emerged that he had many impressions, ideas, and general theories, and they were all fascinating and important. He always, then and later, dismissed this sort of thing as lightweight chatter. When he sometimes wrote pieces that were descriptive, such as his introductions to his collections of Bab Feirtéar's stories, or articles recounting his collecting experiences with Micheál Ó Gaoithín, they were among his more accessible and interesting writing. Sadly, he didn't understand what people saw in these pieces, and he himself thought nothing of them. There was no problem to be solved, no evidence to be sifted forensically, and thus no intellectual challenge.

For the Finnish tour, he could have simply described his experiences in Ireland as head of the Department of Irish Folklore, or of his collecting in Kerry. Those two papers would have been simple to compose and would have been exactly what was needed. He could have taken articles or lectures previously written and recast them. Shortcuts are what invitations like this demand.

Instead, he compiled a list of six different topics, each one focusing on a minute question of historic connection: was there an Irish–Icelandic connection as regards the legend 'Midwife to the Fairies'? What is the history of 'The Man Who Married the Mermaid' in Ireland and Scandinavia? That sort of thing.

He could have – in due course he did – written these papers, methodically and meticulously. But he had limited time. He was preoccupied with personal issues – my thesis, the question of marriage – and administrative problems: retiring staff, lack of funding for the department, new plans to expand the department, to obtain better and more suitable premises, which involved many meetings and eventually came to nothing – a pattern that was to be repeated again and again in UCD. Much squealing and little wool, as the man said when he sheared the pig.

He sat in his flat, with his typewriter, throwing papers in the bin.

The date of the tour came closer and closer and he had not written a single lecture.

I tried to advise. Write about collecting in Kerry. Regurgitate some old lectures.

He looked at me in puzzlement. Who would want to hear about such things? And how could he write about them anyway?

He went back to the psychiatrist.

He took pills.

These were dull days.

Despair was setting in, for me as for him.

I was twenty-eight. I had a doctorate and I was a librarian – not my career of choice, but the work in the National Library was getting more and more interesting.

Now, when I should have been looking forward to getting married, Bo was depressed.

He sat in the evenings with tears in his eyes. The lecture tour loomed like a guillotine. Finland became a dark cloud hanging over the flat in Booterstown. The prospect of the lecture tour, which should have been a joy, invaded our lives like a poison gas, which paralysed Bo, that swift-moving, light-hearted creature.

I tried to push away the monster that is depression. Gradually I found I couldn't. It was almost as if Bo didn't want it to lift, although that was not the case. But that is how someone else's depression can look to those who are closest to them. Why can't they shake it off?

In this instance, I think Bo wanted someone to shift the burden for him, to get him off the hook of Finland. And of the marriage? Was that the real issue? Sometimes what the client believes to be the problem is just displacing the real problem, a psychoanalyst told me, years later.

After a month, I thought I could not go through with the marriage anyway. I couldn't be with someone who was so depressed, so immobile, so unable or unwilling to get out of it. I would have to end up a spinster librarian, after all the Arctic exploring.

But no.

Bo decided to go into hospital.

His doctor had asked him if he wanted to.

According to Bo, he left everything to the patient. If Bo wanted to be admitted to a psychiatric hospital, he would sign the paper. If he didn't, that was okay too.

I knew nothing about psychiatric hospitals, who was admitted and who was not. If I had, I would have realised that the doctor did not think Bo was a very serious case. If he had, there would have been no question of choice. But Bo was not suicidal, for instance. His sense of duty to the Department of Irish Folklore was such that he would never be suicidal while he was in charge there.

I advised him to go to hospital.

We both knew one thing: the moment he was admitted to hospital he could cancel the lecture tour without guilt. It would be the perfect excuse.

Bo was admitted to St Patrick's Hospital. He was given medication which made him sleep for three days.

I went to visit him, in his little room in the old building.

When the aggressive medication was finished, when he emerged from his sleep, he was his old cheerful self. He had his tape recorder, his books. By the end of the week, he was sitting up, working.

I brought fruit, sweets.

He smoked his pipe and after ten days was allowed out for walks. We strolled along the quays, and into the dark old streets around the hospital. Viking Dublin. Arbour Hill, Stoneybatter – places that were unfamiliar to us southsiders, and which I found fascinating and exciting.

It was spring. The trees in the city were veiled in their lovely lime green leaves. The spring was coming back to Bo's step.

In three weeks, he decided to leave the hospital. The depression had lifted like a cloud being blown away by a fresh breeze on a sunny day.

We bought an engagement ring in a jeweller's shop on Nassau Street and began to plan our marriage.

He was never depressed again for the rest of his life.

Bo insisted on getting a house first.

I would have preferred to live in the flat for a while, take our time about choosing a house. But I knew he didn't like the flat and so I compromised. We looked at four or five or six houses, in Stillorgan, Booterstown and Blackrock.

I assumed Bo knew a lot about this sort of thing. He must have known more than me, since I'd never house-hunted before in my life, and he had bought at least four homes so far in his, in various countries and places. But he wasn't much wiser than I was when it came to this task.

He wanted to choose the house, then sell his flat. 'Can't the two transactions be married?' he asked the estate agent, a stocky, belligerent man called Brad.

'We can try,' Brad said.

The housing market was very sluggish in 1982. It was very difficult to sell, so it was a buyer's market. Bo and I, both permanently employed, he with a large salary and I with a reasonable one, were well placed to get a mortgage. We had no difficulty in obtaining the go-ahead. The question was, how much?

Memory does not store all experience.

I have no memory of meetings with the building society, although there must have been at least one. I have no memory of the discussions about mortgages – how much could we have borrowed? Was it twice the man's salary, the woman's not taken into account? I have no memory of how much Bo's salary was at that time. I think I was earning about £10,000. Between leaving the library in 1978 and return in 1982 salaries had increased significantly. And I got increments for my MPhil and PhD.

I remember a few houses we viewed.

One on the Stillorgan Road, near RTÉ and Belfield. A big house with five bedrooms, a garden that backed on to Elm Park Golf Club. There was a bar in the front room.

This house cost £74,000. We thought it was too much. Our limit was about £60,000.

Another house on Booterstown Avenue, not far from Bo's apartment. Four bedrooms. A blocky, ugly house, empty. It was within our price range but dismissed as not looking right.

An estate agent whom we knew as a friend, because she was the daughter of one of Bo's former colleagues, wanted to show us a house in Dundrum. 'You really should see it,' she said. 'They have done such wonderful things to it.'

No. For some reason we didn't want to live in Dundrum. We

didn't pay attention to her advice. Didn't even go to look at the house.

I saw a picture I liked, of a house in Shankill. It had the small panes of glass in the window. Neo-Georgian. One Saturday morning in early June we drove out to look at it, with Brad. The house when we stepped inside it was small and dark. Not suitable.

'We have another one around the corner,' Brad said.

I had seen the photo. Seafield. In the photo it looked ugly, the gable to the road, nothing in it that appealed to me at all.

But we drove around to see it.

What the ad had not said was that Seafield was on the seafront.

We drove around the corner of Corbawn Lane. In front of us, the Irish Sea, blue and sparkling. Dalkey Island. The Hill of Killiney.

Wow!

By comparison with the house we had just viewed, this one was spacious. It had a big, generous front room, looking out over the sea. The floor was solid wood, maple or oak or something like that. There was a dining room opening off the sitting room, a kitchen of a reasonable size at the back. A downstairs cloakroom, and decent bathroom. One very big bedroom at the front of the house, with the sea view.

'This can be the library!' said Bo.

A smaller room overlooking the back garden would be a study for me.

The garden itself was big, shaded by trees in their early summer beauty: big sycamores at the end. A weeping willow, a copper beech, a strange twisted tree covered in yellow blossom that remained unidentified – a Siberian pea tree, I later discovered. In the middle of the garden were two rhododendron bushes, in full flower: bright brilliant pink blossoms enticed the beholder.

'Impressed?' Brad sized up our reactions.

'We like it,' I said.

'How much is it?' Bo asked.

'£60,000. But make me an offer.'

From Brad, that was an invitation to offer less, probably much less. But neither Bo nor I understood the code.

We offered £60,000.

We knew absolutely nothing about the area. It was ten miles from town, but close to the train station. 'You'll be in in half an hour,' the owner told us. He didn't add that the train ran only twice or three times a day and that the last one left town at 6 p.m.

I asked my friend, Mary, who was a town planner, for advice. She gave it with caution.

'My colleague who works out there thought the price was a bit high. He hasn't seen the house, though.' She paused and added, 'It's near a county council estate.'

This could have been interpreted as 'The house is much too expensive and it is in a dodgy area.' But I didn't interpret it like that. I didn't know about council estates and what they meant for property values in the Dublin suburbs. I took the advice at face value.

Our offer was accepted. That was on a Wednesday. The next day the house was advertised in the property supplement in the *Irish Times* for £55,000. Obviously it had been impossible to pull the ad in time. We then withdrew our offer of £60,000 and offered £54,000.

You could have bought almost anything anywhere in Dublin for that money in 1982. In Ranelagh or Dalkey or Ballsbridge. Killiney. Fashionable areas that were going to become ever more fashionable, where property values would increase enormously.

We didn't know anything about property, values, desirable neighbourhoods. We loved the sea view, and the willow tree and the big sycamores, the rhododendrons in the big back garden. We overlooked the basic kitchen, a damp patch on the sitting room wall, the functional 1960s exterior: seaside bungalow.

That it was far from the city centre we saw as a minor problem. All my life I had lived within walking distance of Grafton Street.

I wanted to get away from the area I had grown up in, Ranelagh – poised to become the most desirable place to live in Dublin. Bo had also lived there, when he first came to Ireland. His memories of it were far from happy.

So we bought the house in Seafield, which was called Cala D'Or. Sometime in July we signed the papers, and in early August moved in.

We decided to have a quiet wedding. We went back to Sweden, and married in our favourite city, Uppsala, in December 1982, at a small ceremony attended by Bo's brother and sister and a few friends. His sister and brother were the sponsors. After the wedding, in the registry office, we had dinner in a famous old restaurant, looking out over the English Park, covered in snow. What did I wear? A dark blue suit, designed by John Rocha, still an exclusive, expensive designer in those days. It had a tight jacket with puff sleeves, and a skirt gathered into a blue leather cummerbund. A white lacy blouse and a blue hat with a feather. The suit was stylish, slightly avant-garde, flattering. 'Now that's clothes!' someone said, when I wore it to a party some months later. It was the kind of outfit I could wear again and again.

But dark blue? For my wedding? What a strange choice.

Ever since, I have regretted not wearing white, which would have looked so perfect in the snowy landscape of Sweden.

About a month after the wedding, back at work in the National Library, I ate a sandwich at a new cafe on Molesworth Street. I usually went out to lunch, in some cafe in town, rather than sensibly and frugally eating in the tea room of the Library, which was a smoky shabby prefab in the yard at the bottom of Leinster Lane. I loved walking around Grafton Street, Stephen's Green, Dawson Street, having a look in the shops, picking up bargains, and eating in some cafe, usually on my own, although I regularly met friends for lunch in the Kilkenny Shop or the Alliance Française. Cafes were always springing up and closing down in Dublin in the eighties, recession or no recession, just as they are today.

It was a tasty sandwich, bacon and avocado. But in the middle of the night I felt extremely sick, as nauseous as I ever had been. I vomited profusely during the night and the next day. I was convinced that I had been poisoned by the sandwich. There was no possibility of going to work the next day, and in the evening I went to the doctor. She agreed that it could be food poisoning. Then she asked if there was any chance that I could be pregnant.

'It's very unlikely,' I said

But she did a pregnancy test. A week later she telephoned me with the result. I was at my desk in the National Library.

Positive.

I telephoned Bo from the coin box in the hall of the library, which was more private than the room that I shared with several other librarians.

'*Jag är gravid*,' I told him in Swedish.

'*Va säger du?*' he didn't understand.

'I'm pregnant.'

He laughed and whooped.

'*Du är havande.*'

The old-fashioned way of saying you are pregnant, in Swedish. In his day they didn't say 'gravid'. Just as we usen't to use the word 'pregnant', but some euphemism. 'In the family way'. 'Expecting'.

What surprised me most was the discovery that, during all those years, the pill, while I had been on it, and the condoms, had really worked. I had always used contraceptives but never really believed in their efficacy. They looked so flimsy and unreliable. But I became pregnant the minute we stopped using them. We, who looked so stiff and bookish, were very lucky in that way. Nine months after our wedding, almost to the day, our first son was born. Two years later, we had a second boy. The lights of my life.

'The Battle of Ventry'

Bo's last Thursday on earth was a sparkling gem of a day.

I was doing another interview. Halloween week, the season of radio shows about folklore. In the old days, on Halloween, the *sidhe* or the raths opened and the fairies sneaked out, the graves opened and the dead walked the countryside. Now the radio producers' minds open and they want to talk about old customs, old ways, old tales. This time it was to be a panel discussion on storytelling. It would take place from three to four in the afternoon, in RTÉ. I was going to say something about the kind of stories we told in Ireland. The challenge in these discussions is to say something that is true, but not too complex. People expect you to describe stories as if there were only a few, or a few kinds, while there are hundreds of thousands, and many different genres. It is like being asked to describe Irish literature in a line or two. Impossible. But that is the challenge.

I thought I should have a few examples. One of the stories I like to tell is 'The Man Who Had No Story'. Once when I asked Bo what his favourite Irish folk tale was, he said it was this particular one. It's a story that illustrates the importance of storytelling in the Irish community. As the title indicates, it's about a man who has no story, but who goes on an outing, has some strange experiences, and comes home with a story to tell. But I knew – for some reason – I should mention Fenian tales and I didn't really know any very well. I consulted Seán Ó Conaill's Book – I think – or some other collection. I read 'The Battle of Ventry'. Wrote a few notes.

Went to the hospital.

It was about noon. Bo seemed much the same, perhaps a little weaker. The bag of urine was depressingly light. The drip was dripping much faster than it had been, and I realised that it was not functioning properly at all last night when I was visiting, and perhaps for the entire night after that. Who would have checked? The doctors on their rounds this morning.

Bo's voice was weaker. His stomach was more swollen. His ankles were swollen. Oedema. I pointed this out to a nurse. She shrugged and did not seem unduly concerned.

He was lying back and had little energy.

I told him I'd leave for a few hours in the afternoon, that I was doing an interview on RTÉ about storytelling. Kelly Fitzgerald, with whom I had collaborated on Halloween night, a week earlier, would also be on it. I said I had been trying to tell 'The Battle of Ventry'.

'Never try to tell "The Battle of Ventry",' Bo said, with a flare of his sharp humour, but in such a weakened voice. 'It is a terrible story.'

'Which one should I tell?'

'"Fionn in the Cradle" is good,' he said. He began to tell it but gave up before the end, although it's a short tale.

Lunch was served. Fish and potatoes and soup. He waved it away. The sight of food made him feel sick – he probably felt very sick all the time. There was a dessert, jelly and ice cream, and I fed him a little of that. I gave him drinks of water but now, for the first time, a nurse came and told me not to. The drip was enough. At two I left, took the 145 to RTÉ, and did the interview. After the recording, the producer told us it would be broadcast on 28 December, after Christmas. A question popped up in my mind, out of nowhere, out of fear that was obviously gripping me then, although in the hospital they were saying Bo would be fine. I asked myself this: Will he be alive when this programme is broadcast? I could not imagine what it would be like, if he were not.

Kelly, who is a very warm, kind young woman, walked along the road with me towards the bus stop. She told me that Brenda Ennis, the author of *The Secret of the Sleeveen,* which I had launched just one week earlier on Halloween, was very anxious to meet me, to give me a present. I knew this since Brenda had mentioned it to me on the night of the launch. I explained that Bo was in hospital, so for the moment I'd rather not make an arrangement to meet. Maybe in a week or so. Kelly was surprised, and rather alarmed, but I calmed her down and said it was nothing serious, he would be fine soon. I said this. I still believed this. Bo was at the end of his trial period. Actually he was past the end, so why wasn't I hearing about the next phase of treatment? They would try something else now.

Back at the hospital, there was a new development. Bo was wheezing. I saw a young doctor, the night doctor, who looked like an intern. She gave him a nebuliser, which helped his breathing and seemed to give him some energy.

That evening, Marja, Ragnar, Olaf and Nadezhda, came to visit. Again we were quite a crowd in the ward, and there were no seats for anyone. Nadezhda had brought a little tub of fresh fruit – melon, grapes, pineapple – and she fed some of this to Bo. She knew he loved melon. He ate it.

We were cheerful. Bo was glad to see everyone. Two nights before, when he was stronger, much stronger, he had looked at the departing Ragnar and Marja and Olaf with pride, and said how well they looked, intimated that he was glad that he had such presentable children. Now he could not say that but he enjoyed having them around his bed, and talked excitedly, at length, but in such a weak voice that we couldn't really hear what he was saying.

We left obediently at about nine. Marja offered to spend the night in Shankill, with me, and I was glad of the company. We drank some wine and talked about strategies. Marja and Ragnar would get an appointment with the consultant the following morning, and persuade him that Bo should be moved to a hospital where he would be more comfortable. They would be calmer and better negotiators than I could be, I knew, and I felt reassured. My plan was to drop Marja up to the hospital, then go to UCD and teach my Friday class. I would not get back to the hospital until about five. But Marja and Ragnar would be there, and with luck Bo would be moving to a better hospital.

'They're closing down the A&E in Loughlinstown in a few weeks,' Marja said. 'It was on the news last night.'

I laughed. If Bo had fallen ill a few weeks later he could not have been taken there. He was among the last cohort of patients that were ever admitted to that A&E.

We went to bed at about midnight. At half past twelve, my mobile rang. I had a moment of panic. The hospital.

The call was from Bo's mobile, which he very seldom used, although I had called him a few times in the hospital on it, since he had no bedside phone, needless to say. Indeed there was no telephone access to patients except by way of their own mobiles. But although the screen told me the phone was Bo's a nurse spoke first.

'Your husband asked me to phone. He wants to speak to you.'

She gave the phone to Bo.

'Hi darling, what's up?' I asked.

'I am in such terrible pain,' Bo said. He emphasised the word 'pain'. 'They don't understand what I am saying.'

'I'll go up there,' I said.

'No no no no no!' he shouted, insofar as he could shout. 'Do not come up here. Talk to them.'

'Okay, okay,' I said. 'I'll talk to them. Take it easy now, darling, I love you.'

I spoke to the nurse.

'He is in terrible pain,' I said.

'I will give him some painkillers,' she said.

'Ring me if anything happens,' I said.

'He will be all right. He has been agitated.'

What do they mean when they say a patient has been agitated? Do they mean he has been shrieking with pain? Begging for help?

'I will ring you if there is anything.'

I went downstairs and told Marja. I wondered if I should go to the hospital. But I had had two glasses of wine, I didn't think I should drive.

But couldn't I have risked it, for once?

Couldn't I have got a taxi?

I was going to teach in the morning. I was still in ordinary time, watching the clock. I still didn't get it.

I went back to bed.

The Last of April

I had seen the rafts being built by students. An igloo, made of white fibreboard. A flying saucer. *The Simpsons* and Donald Duck. The rafts were under construction on the bank of the River Fyris during the last week of April. Between the clear, fresh birch trees and the sparkling water where the ducks paddled they sat, waiting to be finished. The apartment where we always stayed in Uppsala, belonging to Bo's brother Hugo, was in a block on the bank of the river and so I saw the rafts as I walked along the path into the centre of town, just a few minutes downstream. They looked amazing: they were imaginative and witty and meaningful, but as well as all that they were seaworthy, or at least riverworthy. That students of literature and medicine and history, that any student at all, could make such things impressed me immensely. I longed to see the rafts on the water sailing down the river. But for some reason we always went home before that happened. On the Last of April. That's what Bo, and therefore I, called it – *Sista April* – although I noticed that people called it *Valborgsmässoafton,* Walpurgis Night. Uppsala was Bo's city. But he had left the country in 1970. Now he was out of touch with the idioms of the day. The basic language had not changed, of course, but the slang had, and so had a lot of the usages. They said things that he had told me were incorrect, impossible: like *Jag älsker glass,* I love ice cream. When he was a young man, you could only use the verb 'to love' about a person. People would think you ridiculous if you announced that you loved a thing. There was another expression for that. But now you could love ice cream, or a new frock, or a movie, just as in English.

In 2013 I decided we would finally be in Uppsala for the Last of April. Bo had talked so much about it; for years, decades, I had longed to be there on the big day. It was the biggest festival in the university town, when the students went wild. They all gathered in the big square in front of the library, Carolina Rediviva. The president of the university, called Rektor Magnificus, made a speech from a balcony. Then he put on his student cap, a white velvet cap with a black visor, like a sailor's. And all the thousands of students donned their own caps, and ran like a river down the hill, Carolinabacken, down to ... well, the river. And then they celebrated, with beer and *snaps* and champagne, and did crazy things. Once, my husband said, he – a student then – had walked across the high balustrade of the Iron Bridge at midnight, endangering his life, just for fun. That was the sort of thing that went on.

We flew to Sweden on the second last day of April, 2013. We stayed in Stockholm overnight, with our son Ragnar and his wife, Ailbhe, who were living there at the time. Hugo had died in 2011, a few weeks short of his hundredth birthday, so we had no family apartment waiting for us in Uppsala, as had been the case for thirty years, since we got married in the city, from that apartment, in 1982.

On the last of April we got the 10.10 train to Uppsala from Central Station. We were lucky to get a seat because it was packed to capacity with young people. They carried bottles of wine and beer, and backpacks. A particularly beautiful girl, with long shining fair hair and enormous eyes, uncorked a bottle of wine and began swigging from it, right there on the train. A few boys drank from beer cans but most of the young folk just chatted and laughed. The train, which I usually thought of as a sedate, sombre train, carrying soberly dressed academic types, with their noses stuck in a book or a laptop, was full of the sound of youthful giddiness. I observed it all with what I thought of as anthropological interest, or just curiosity. Bo read his book, as he always did, on trains, planes, buses, in waiting rooms, oblivious to the noise around him.

We were greeted at the station by hundreds of policemen, in their navy uniforms and jaunty caps, carrying batons and guns. The hordes of students from Stockholm poured out of the station, past the cycle park where thousands of bicycles stood, and into the wide street in front of the station. Like all streets beside big railway stations, it was dull and faintly depressing, but unlike most of them it wasn't shabby. The young people moved in a mass up the street that led to the big square, the river, and, on the other bank, the massive old university on the hill. We walked along the railway street. Our hotel was somewhere along there near Linnégatan. For the first time in my life I would sleep in a hotel in Uppsala. I was excited at the prospect. Bo found it discomfiting. It emphasised the change in our lives, reminded him that his beloved older brother was dead and that we no longer had a relative in Uppsala.

The Last of April.

The beginning of spring in Sweden. The long white nights were starting, May could be a lovely month up here in the north. But today the thermostat in the hotel registered seven degrees, and the sky was full of edgy clouds, scuttling about threateningly. When I was a child I experienced real sadness when a picnic day turned out cold and rainy. In spite of experience, I would cling to the hope that the sun would come out, that we would sit on the grass in the country, or by the sea, our table flooded with splendid sunlight, that everything would be as it should be. Now I felt a slight tinge of that same disappointment with the elements. But just a tinge. Those small hopes and disappointments become much less acute as one gets older. Also, I had found that when I was with Bo I just didn't feel such disappointments anyway, about big things or bad things. Bad weather? We would laugh at it. Once I was with him, I felt okay about life – protected, because he knew what to do in most situations, and also had that enthusiastic optimistic personality that is like the heat of the sun.

Uppsala, I liked to think, was one of my cities. (I liked that phrase, 'my city', which I had read in someone's memoir, in the sentence, 'Dublin is my city.') Uppsala is my city too, because I was married in it, on a snowy winter's day, and I had visited it maybe twenty times since then. Also, I loved it, because it was beautiful and old and very Swedish. I knew all the streets from Torsgatan, where Hugo's flat was, to the English Park, at the far side of town. Every day, during my visits, I walked all the way along the river, past the Uppland Museum and the cathedral, past the shops and old hotels, past the English Park and the hospital, to the yard where people kept their boats and yachts. In summer they would sail along the river into the great lake Mälaren, and then on into Stockholm and the sea. Or so I imagined. I knew, in particular, the shops: the nice little boutique on St Olof's Gata where you could get expensive clothes, linen and undyed wool; Hemtex, for tablecloths and textiles; the big department store, Åhléns. It was as familiar to me as Dublin or Dingle, and I enjoyed it more because it was always exotic.

On the Last of April, though, it felt strange, and I felt like a foreigner. There were always lots of students in the city, of course, cycling and walking. It actually was their city; it's like Oxford, a city that belongs to students. But now it was crammed. The shops were closed and the cafes were packed so getting a bite to eat would be a challenge. The hotel we were staying in was fine, but its restaurant was called MacFie's; the seats were covered with red tartan and the TVs screened football matches from the UK.

Before trying to get lunch, we walked down to the river, where the raft race was on.

The river in Uppsala is its great treasure, at least as precious as the medieval cathedral or the six-hundred-year-old university. The river is older – of course – and even more beautiful. The many bridges are picturesque, some ancient and some new.

The water passes slowly under some of them. At other places, it dashes along in rapids over rocks and bumps.

It was on the rapids that the raft race took place.

We stood on the street opposite the museum and a Greek restaurant with an outdoor area looking down over the river, where we had eaten many times over the past thirty years. At this point the river ran downhill for about half a kilometre, over rocks, in a series of rapids, and this was where the rafts were sailing. It was different from what I had imagined. (Everything is.) I had envisioned the rafts sailing peacefully along the calm stretches of the river, down through the streets and the park. But no, they were being set off, in twos and threes, from a point above a little waterfall, to shoot the rapids. Two ambulances were positioned just above the Greek restaurant, waiting for eventual casualties. Lifeguards, in wetsuits with underwater regalia, stood in the water at either side.

A raft with an igloo on top came hopping and skipping down the rapids. The crowd cheered. The goal was, I understood, to make it over the rapids without capsizing or falling into the water.

'Did you do this?'

'No.' He smiled.

'I wonder when they started doing it?'

He didn't answer. He hadn't been in the city on the Last of April in over forty years. Time and space have different dimensions but sometimes one can relate them. Forty years is further away in time than Ireland is from Sweden in distance. Very much further. Even in the Viking days, in the early Middle Ages, they would get from Norway to Dublin in a week or so, spend the summer raiding and robbing, and return home. Two weeks on the North Sea. These days two and a half hours in the air takes you from Dublin to Stockholm. And vice versa. In history there is no vice versa; it is a one-way flight, no return possible.

It started to spit rain, and sleet. People, well wrapped up in thick, dark, waterproof coats, were moving away from the river.

The igloo was manned by two students. It came shooting down the river and they stayed on board. Then it floated fairly serenely along the calmer water towards the finishing line, or whatever it was.

'Would you like to go and get some lunch?'

'Whatever you want, darling.'

It was all for me, this day, this Last of April. Being back in his beloved old city to revisit the highlight of the student year meant nothing to Bo. Or it meant something that was not enjoyable, maybe painful. I didn't really know what, though.

I wanted to see one more.

The next raft was already coming down. This one had a fairy-tale castle with icicles dripping from it and there was only one skipper. It shot over the rapids, tumbling and turning, and when it flew into the deeper water the student was tossed overboard. Everyone screamed 'Ah!' I felt excited. I knew they all did. This was what we all wanted to see, really – people falling off their rafts, into the icy water. Without a second's hesitation the lifeguard threw the buoy out, and one of the divers swam rapidly to where the student had disappeared into the black water. I watched eagerly. He – or she – would be rescued. There was no doubt. There was only a fraction of a doubt. If it was really dangerous they wouldn't be allowed do it.

Yes. He ... or she ... was rescued, and we went off looking for a place to eat.

After lunch we went up to the library, Carolina Rediviva. A huge crowd was gathered, old people as well as young. Champagne on trays, picnics. A choir singing 'Gaudeamus Igitur' and many other songs.

There were hailstones, but spirits were high.

At three o'clock the Rektor Magnificus, who was a Rektor Magnifica this time, made her little speech and donned her cap.

And all the caps went on, on young and old, although not on Bo. In Dublin he would put on his student cap on the Last of April, but not here.

That was that.

'Don't they run down the hill?'

Not any more. It's not permitted for safety reasons. It would be lethal nowadays, with so many students. That custom too had bitten the dust. Everything changes, and if you are an emigrant, you find these changes abrupt and disturbing. You are a stranger in your own country and your own city. You return to it from another place and from another time.

Lingon was Bo's favourite restaurant in Uppsala. He belonged to a generation of Swedish men who always ate in restaurants if they were unmarried. As a student, his allowance had permitted him to do this – there were cheap places to eat, then, the 'Nations', which are a kind of student club associated with the various Swedish counties, and endowed to some extent by alumni (Bo's nation was Värmlands Nation). In Dublin, when Bo lived alone in Booterstown, he always ate a three-course lunch in the staff restaurant in Belfield, and a three-course dinner in the Tara Towers Hotel on the Rock Road. Of course, in Shankill we always had dinner at home. I like cooking, and, in the years after the boys left home, when it was just the two of us in the house, dinner was a pleasant ritual. I cooked, we ate by candlelight with a glass of wine, chatted and lingered. Bo always took care of the washing-up and filling and emptying the dishwasher. In the early days of our marriage I had grumbled that he never cooked. My feminist principles demanded that he should. It was not entirely true that he never cooked. When left alone with the boys he could rustle up a meal of potatoes, salad, and either pork chops or meatballs. They, in fact, preferred his meatballs – nothing but meat, fried to a crisp – to anything I cooked. As we had more time, and mellowed, I accepted that I enjoyed cooking and stopped complaining. I got the best of the bargain anyway – washing-up is not half as much fun as cooking.

Tonight, Lingon was operating a special deal. They had installed an outdoor barbecue, and there were only two things on the menu, lamb or salmon. There was a long queue waiting to be served. We stood in the cold wondering if it was worth it. But we were not standing for long when a man, perhaps attached to the restaurant, said to the maître d', 'Haven't you got a table for the professor?'

'Do you know us?' I asked.

'No, but I know what a professor looks like.'

We were both pleased. Bo still looked like a professor, an Uppsala professor, in his eighty-first year. A handsome Uppsala professor – he looked like a character in a Bergman film.

And we got a table.

We visited an old friend in Uppsala on 1 May, Ingrid, and had lunch in her lovely apartment before going back to Stockholm. Although we were seeing various friends and relatives, and doing a bit of sightseeing, the main reason for this trip to Sweden, the main reason, was that Bo was getting his passport renewed. The Swedish Embassy in Ireland had closed some years earlier, and now Swedish citizens living in Ireland have to go to London or Stockholm. Due to new security regulations it is quite a complex procedure and was not comfortable – long queues, confusion because Bo had an Irish address, a general inefficiency that was not characteristic of Sweden but confirmed our suspicion that life would be easier if there was an embassy in Dublin. But finally we got the passport, valid for ten more years.

There were a few more stages to our holiday. We went south on the train from Stockholm to Ystad, home of Kurt Wallander, the fictional detective created by Henning Mankell, whose writing I love. From Ystad, we were going to the island of Bornholm, which neither of us had ever visited, and then on to Copenhagen before returning home.

In Ystad we stayed in a hostel that was based in the old Custom House, which had been used in the first TV series based on the Wallander novels. Our room was the one that had been Svartman's office in the first few series of the drama. Like all the Swedish hostels, this one was more like a hotel, simple but comfortable. It did not serve food, however, and we had dinner in one of Wallander's favourite restaurants, Opp och När.

Our day in Ystad was a bright sunny one. The town is old and very picturesque, with narrow streets of pretty wooden houses, a medieval monastery, flowerbeds full of dazzling flowers – thousands of purple and yellow pansies, Bo's favourites because they are so cheerful, always smiling. A river, a duck pond, ducks. The television drama, intent on revealing the dark side of Sweden, conveys little or no impression of the charm and beauty of the town and the surrounding landscape.

Bo and I walked around, but his back ached and he spent most of the day sitting outside a cafe, reading, while I explored the shops. I went to my favourite department store, Åhléns, where I set off the alarm as I walked in the door.

This had happened a few times on the holiday, this sudden setting-off of alarms. Nobody could figure out what was causing it. But now, in the town of Wallander, a young male assistant solved the problem. Was I possibly carrying something in my handbag that had not been desensitised. Make-up? I opened my bag, fished out a lipstick, and he desensitised it.

How had it got there?

A lipstick bought in Dunne's Stores. Or perhaps not bought? Left by mistake at the bottom of the trolley, never paid for or checked out? It could have happened, I couldn't swear that it had not.

The alarms could have been omens. But there was a rational explanation.

There were other possible omens. I dreamt that my teeth were falling out. Some people believe that this dream, which many have, heralds a death. But I was having problems with my teeth. There was a boil in my mouth, a gumboil, which would not heal, in spite of applications of Bonjela and other medications. I interpreted my dream about teeth falling out as a dream about teeth. And when I got back to Dublin and had it checked it was discovered that I had an infected root. Root canal work was tried and failed. Sometime in September – much later – the tooth was extracted.

Bo, long ago when we were young and having our very first holiday together in Denmark, told a story about Bornholm. As a young man he was going to a nightclub in Nyhavn in Copenhagen with his Icelandic friend, Eggert. They both spoke Danish and claimed to be Danish. A Dane they were drinking with looked suspiciously at Bo and said '*Enten er du svensk, eller er du frå Bornholm.*'

Bo had expressed a wish to go to Bornholm then, and often afterwards. In recent years, a Danish friend, Lis Pihl, whose father came from Bornholm, and who visited it from time to time, encouraged us to visit the island with her for a few days. Yes, we would, we would. But Lis died in 2011, from ovarian cancer, and we never made that trip – a matter that I had always regretted.

But now we were on our way.

We were on the big ferry, sailing over the Baltic to the little island that lies between Sweden and Germany but belongs to Denmark. And, just as was the case on the Last of April in Uppsala, Bo was not all that interested in the experience. He appeared to have forgotten that once he had longed to see Bornholm. But now, although he did not express any indifference, I could see that he didn't care about it much one way or the other. All the enthusiasm for the voyage was mine. Perhaps Bo would have preferred to go to Gothenburg, and visit his sister Vera? She is eleven years his senior. There was always the risk that we would not see her again, that she would die before our next visit. Or perhaps his travelling days were over. All his life he had been a traveller, an explorer. But that impulse was fading. He no longer cared about seeing new places. I've read in a memoir by one of my favourite writers, Penelope Lively, that, in her eighties, she no longer had any desire to travel abroad, although all her life she had loved going to new places. The desire had disappeared, and travel abroad seemed to be more trouble than it was worth. In Bo I had seen over the past few years that the old excitement was no longer there. It was as if he was already moving out of the world, and that the places on planet Earth that we love, for their beauty or history (always more of a draw, for him), were losing their lustre and significance.

We arrived in Rønne, the capital, and took a bus to Svaneke. Lis Pihl always stayed in this village, at a hotel called Siemsens Gaard. I had booked a few nights there, partly to honour Lis's memory and partly because I knew it was a good hotel.

It's an old merchant's house close to the harbour in Svaneke, which is a picturesque old village, with timbered houses, rose-filled gardens. We arrived at about 9 p.m. The restaurant in the hotel had stopped serving food; none of the other Svaneke restaurants were open. Tomorrow would be Ascension Thursday, a bank holiday in Sweden and Denmark, but the holiday season had not started yet. In the only pub that was open – a convivial place where we were made to feel very welcome by the few customers – we had a beer and a packet of peanuts, the only food on sale. Laughing, we went home, rather hungry, to bed in our simple, comfortable room.

Next day we took the bus that goes around the coastline of Bornholm. Windmills, green fields, pretty old houses. It didn't take very long to reach Rønne, which is a big enough town, and not enchanting. Ordinary. In the bookshop, Bo bought a book about Bornholm and over lunch he told me the story of the end of the Second World War on the island. On 7 May 1945, when the people of Copenhagen were celebrating the end of the war and of occupation by Germany, Bornholm, still under the command of a diehard German officer, was bombed by the Russians. For a year, the island was held by Russia, while its fate was decided: would it become part of the Eastern Bloc, or stay Danish? In the event, it remained with Denmark, of course. But Bornholm felt betrayed by the Danes and has never forgotten this episode – from which its tourist industry makes plenty of mileage these days.

We didn't go to a museum. This was one of the great aspects of travelling with Bo. He knew the history of almost every place we ever visited, and enthralled me with stories of those places, but we did not always feel it was essential to see all the tourist spots. Being with him as a travelling companion was almost like being alone – except a million times better. I always felt that we were at our best, as a couple, travelling together. We rhymed with one another, as we walked and flew and sailed. And we had many perfect journeys together.

It is not that our interests always coincided precisely. Sometimes I liked to be more active than Bo, especially in these later years, when his backache prevented him from walking as much as had been his custom for most of his life. I had dreamed of cycling on Bornholm – a flat island, filled with small country roads. A Swedish friend of mine from my Copenhagen days, Ulla, had spent a holiday once with her mother on the island cycling around, and based on her descriptions I had imagined an idyllic experience. And the island is certainly ideal for cycling: flat. There are cycle paths everywhere and anyway not much traffic. The hotel had bicycles that one could borrow. I set off. In practice it was not as wonderful as I imagined. The skies were overcast, the island was quiet, empty, a bit gloomy. I cycled in one direction, then in another. Photographed a windmill. Followed a sign saying Paradise Bakken. Who would not? But Paradise Bakken turned out to be a camping site on the top of perhaps the only hill on Bornholm, a forested slope. As often when hiking or cycling alone I began to feel the place was a bit creepy. After a few hours cycling, I was back in Siemsens Gaard.

Bo was at home in the hotel room, sitting at the desk, translating an Icelandic saga, a short one, *Bornholms Saga*, to Swedish. He became engrossed in this work of translation, which he always loved. Over the two days he completed the translation and handed me the printout. It was dedicated to me. For Éilís. *Till minna om vår semester på Bornholm.* For Éilís, in memory of our holiday on Bornholm. Back home, he placed it on my desk by my printer. It is there still.

Was it another sign? A sign that Bo was thinking of death? Almost certainly. He had had close brushes with it: his prostate cancer diagnosis and treatment two years earlier, a bowel cancer tumour that had been removed less than a year ago. On this holiday, the ghost of Hugo was with us in Uppsala, and now we remembered Lis Pihl on Bornholm. Bo did not talk about death and we were optimistic about his health. He was strong, and his siblings Hugo and Vera had lived for decades following cancer treatment. Bo had just renewed his passport for another ten years. I am sure he did not know that this was our last holiday abroad together. But I am also sure that he was reflecting on his own mortality. It upset him that he was slowing down – finally at the age of eighty-two. We had celebrated his birthday in Stockholm on 5 May, with Ragnar and Ailbhe and our great friend from Stockholm, Helena Wulff.

We treated each other with unusual gentleness on this holiday. I was very aware of his delicacy – he was not as robust as on all the other holidays, even the recent ones. He needed to rest in the afternoons. He was kind to me, as he always was, and I was kind to him, as I often had not been. He seemed distant, too, as if he was retreating, withdrawing into the shadowy wings of life. I was shy of him, sometimes, on this holiday – as if I did not know him as well as I believed, as if he were becoming a stranger once again, becoming, once again, himself.

And that he dedicated the translation to me touched me to the core.

This is what he used to do in the first days of our love. He wrote a poem, a letter, he sent me poems and books with sweet dedications.

Oh yes, not only in retrospect, not only in geography, was there a sense of a circle closing.

The mood during the few days on Bornholm was new to me. Poignancy, fear of separation, was not in itself new – Bo had had many health scares, I had often been afraid that he would die. And I was not feeling that here. But there was some unfamiliar nuance, some fresh note, in the complex symphony of our relationship. Being pitched together in a hotel room, on a holiday together, on an island, has always engendered a new intimacy, closeness, and tenderness. But this time that tenderness was different. Bo was quieter and more reflective than usual. His pain – the pain in his back – was a constant, and it took him away from me. He did not complain about it though. He was patient, withdrawing into himself. The mystery and reserve that characterised him long ago, before I got to know him, before he was my lover or my husband, seemed to be returning. He was shy, and I was shy too.

In a marriage, two people who are very close, closely engaged with one another, can fade into one. I had always believed myself to be very independent. I travelled alone, often, to conferences and literary events. I attended many social events on my own, and I had a circle of friends who were mine, not Bo's. And he was the same. We had our own lives. Even so, my life, my identity, was very closely linked to his. My sense of myself, of who I was, was grafted on to his character. 'So we grew together,/ Like to a double cherry, seeming parted,/ But yet a union in partition.' Like many married couples, we had learnt to move in harmony, and could read one another's thoughts. But on Bornholm I sensed that Bo was withdrawing, to a place or state that was out of reach to me.

Or could it have been, simply, that he was thinking of all our dead friends? Of Lis Pihl? Just few years ago she was here in

Siemsens Gaard, and she was in Dublin too – just a few months before she died, she came to Dublin for the last time. Or was he thinking of his sister Vera and her husband, in their nineties, in their lovely house outside Gothenburg? Was he thinking he might not see them again, that he had missed his chance?

Denmark and Sweden were countries of the dead, for Bo. His beloved brother died just two years ago, Lis Pihl about the same time. His sister Vesta, his brother Helge, his parents … all gone. For me the focus was still on the living. I had friends in Stockholm and Uppsala and Copenhagen. Our son and his wife in Stockholm. Of course Bo shared these contacts with me, but it may have been that Bornholm, its grey skies, its cool spring weather, its shadows, reminded him of those who had already left the world, and that his time to depart would come. Perhaps he was frightened?

This would have been a time to talk about death. There was tenderness, a gentleness, in the calm harmonious peaceful air of Svaneke that invited intimate discussions. I could have courted my beloved again, and learned to know this new version of him, which was rather like the oldest version, the first version: a man I found utterly attractive, was intrigued by, for whom I had massive respect. A precious, rare type of human being.

We did not, however, talk about serious matters. But perhaps we did not need to. As at the beginning, even before there was any acknowledgement of affection, there was an understanding in the air between us – now in the touch of our hands, in our light kisses and kind goodnights, a similar empathy prevailed. Bo and I were people of the word, but we could communicate without recourse to language too. You do not need to articulate everything. Some feelings are beyond language.

We knew we loved one another, and that was both wondrous, and sad, because in that love was the seed of deep lasting grief.

It could be that he saw this, and feared it. Perhaps he was thinking of me? How would I manage, when he was no longer with me? Who would be my travelling companion then? Surely he could see how much I relished these holidays with him, the pleasure I took in simple things like a day on a train, a night in a hostel? And who was there, in the world, who could share my particular interests: who else would want to stay in the fictional Wallander police station in Ystad? And voyage out to Bornholm, listen to its language, catch the bus to Rønne and decide to leave it just as quickly? Who else knew or cared about the island of Bornholm, its history? About the Last of April? Sweden and Denmark and Iceland and Ireland?

Who else spoke our language? Our mixture of languages, Irish and English and Swedish and German and French? Sometimes all in the same paragraph. Nobody else, that I know.

I worry about Bo. I fear his death, but I can't get past that moment, in my fearsome fantasies, the moment when he will vanish. Maybe it's too painful to imagine what it will be like, life without Bo in it? More likely, I have difficulty imagining absence, nothingness. Imagination creates new worlds: the Brontës' Angria, the fairy *lios*, Heaven and Hell. The concept of zero is alien to it, as it was to the Greek mathematicians. I can imagine dying, because when one is in the process of dying one is still in the land of the living. But I can't imagine *being dead*, I can't imagine the state of non-being. And I couldn't imagine what life without Bo, with Bo dead, not alive, not here, would be like, not in any detail. Because there is no detail in zero.

'There's no point thinking about death,' many old people say. Hugo, Bo's brother, used to say that. 'I can't do anything about it. So I just don't think about it.'

There is no point in thinking about death, or about life without Bo. *Den dagen den sorgen.*

I had never considered the opposite: what life would be like for Bo without me, because of course it was most unlikely that I would go first. Statistics demonstrate that the man usually dies first, and given our age difference the chances were multiplied.

It's possible, though, that he considered what life without him might be like for me. This is something that an older partner, who has had cancer, and has a sore back, might have had on his mind. It's possible that he worried about it, at least now and then. Perhaps that was one of the reasons for his reserve? His shy tenderness, as if he did not really know me very well? Did he sense that this was our last holiday?

Later, I wish we had talked about this, about all these matters. I yearn for more documents and evidence, and less speculation. A letter from Bo would be good, one of those letters of encouragement that the bereaved get in sentimental novels.

It would be nice not to have to make it up, and guess what Bo would have advised me to do with my life after his.

But he didn't write one of those letters. He just handed me the little saga that he has worked on so diligently, in Siemsens Gaard.

Bornholms Saga. 'For Éilís, in memory of our holiday on Bornholm.'

It symbolises everything he has given me – a very great deal.

'The Sod of Death'

Níl fhios ag éinne cá bhfuil fód a bháis

There was a man who lived near here. One day he was out cutting turf near the clifftop. He was working away when he heard a voice coming from the ditch, or the sea, or somewhere. And the voice said, that sod you're cutting is the sod of your death. The man said, no way. He cut the sod, went to the top of the cliff, and tossed it into the sea.

Twenty years later his son was on the beach and he found a huge sod of turf. It had been hardened by the sea. He brought it home and shaped it into a sort of stool, and he put it by the fire. His father sat on it, and the next thing, he keeled over and died.

It was the sod he had cut many years earlier. It came to him, in the end.

First thing on Friday morning, I phoned the hospital. The nurse said Bo had had a bad night, had been agitated.

That word again.

Why do medical professionals not say what they mean? Why do they speak in euphemisms, in vague words that are open to interpretation?

I decided I would not take my class after all, but go directly to the hospital.

Marja telephoned the hospital and asked if she could speak to the consultant. I think they said yes, she should ask for him when she came to the hospital, he would be there in the late morning.

Another glorious autumn day. The trees plated with gold. Blue sky. Not a breath of wind.

At about ten thirty we went to the ward. Bo was surrounded by doctors. The team. We were asked to stand aside for a while and we waited in the corridor at the end of the ward, while the doctors attended to Bo. I was reassured by the fact that at least doctors were attending to him, at last.

What happened over the next few hours, the rest of Friday morning, is a bit of a blur. A young doctor told me that Bo's kidney condition had worsened. I told him he had been chesty and his breathing had weakened last night and I asked, 'Is he about to go into heart failure?'

'He's in heart failure already,' he said.

I thought: Bo went into heart failure at 12.30 last night, when he telephoned me. That was the terrible pain. And the nurse gave him more paracetamol. 'Agitated' can be nurse-speak for heart failure.

'He has to get into Intensive Care' is another thing the doctor said. 'We're trying to get him a bed in our Intensive Care Unit, or else in Vincent's.'

My heart jumped. If only we could get him to Vincent's. If only we had got him to Vincent's on Monday night. It is not that I trust Vincent's University Hospital much. But it is better than Loughlinstown. And the possibility of getting a bed in the private hospital might be greater – at least the two hospitals are on the same campus.

Except now that did not matter because Bo was going to go into Intensive Care.

One of the doctors told me that a person can survive with one quarter kidney function. One eighth of each kidney, he said, that is a quarter.

Hope.

Bo had 100 per cent kidney function a week ago. Now, after a week in this place, we were talking about 25 per cent.

Marja and I went over to Bo's bed and talked to him. He was very weak and tired. I told him they were going to move him to Intensive Care, to help him. Marja asked if he'd like to hear a piece from *Bombi Bitt och Jag*. Bo found a passage and she read a page or so. It was the description of the market, a classic scene in this book, celebrated in Swedish literature. Bo was spreadeagled on the bed, his pyjamas open over his now quite distended stomach. Listening.

I had moved into another zone.

I knew now that a battle was on, for Bo's life, and I knew that I would have to fight this battle – Bo always did, he was strong, brave, resilient. We were in the gap of danger.

The doctor I had seen earlier in the week told us that they were moving Bo to Intensive Care not because he was in any danger but just so they could monitor him better, and another doctor was telling us, again reassuringly, that a person could survive with one quarter of kidney function.

Several doctors spoke to me over the next hour. An argument developed between some of the them about whether Bo should be admitted to Intensive Care Unit there or not. But it emerged that the doctor who was against the idea was looking at the wrong file. There were raised voices and a slammed door.

I was looking on at all this like a small child gawping at an adult conversation.

Now I joined in. 'It's the wrong file! I don't believe this.'

A nice young doctor said, 'He will get into Intensive Care. Don't worry.'

In the shambles that constituted the hospital, there were some people I was grateful for, people who did their best. The young doctors, probably still training. Some of the nurses. I liked the consultant when I finally met him and he did his best to save Bo. But I felt he arrived on the scene too late in the day.

Bo was moved into Intensive Care in Loughlinstown. Possibly, even at that point, if he had been moved to Vincent's things would have turned out differently. Possibly not. Possibly it was already too late.

I, and the other family members, were moved into a tiny waiting room opposite the ICU. It is a small, poky room with a very high ceiling. Painted pea green, it is furnished with two green sofas and a chair. A small coffee table. There is a broken water dispenser in one corner, and the window looks out on another building. It is a grim, cheerless room but by Loughlinstown standards better than any other waiting room, since it has sofas, not plastic stacking chairs.

Bo was moved into Intensive Care at about lunchtime on Friday. We – our numbers were expanding – took up residence in the green waiting room. At this point, the consultant spoke to us.

'We are going to do everything possible for your husband,' he told me. 'Age is not a consideration, we will try everything. If he does not respond to our treatment by three o'clock he will have to have dialysis or partial dialysis.'

I had already been told, on Bo's first day in this hell, that partial dialysis might kick-start Bo's kidney function again. Dialysis did not mean permanent, regular dialysis. It is a good treatment for kidney failure. It probably should have been applied much earlier – before Bo had heart failure, for example.

'Can you do dialysis here?'

Is it the first time I have asked this question?

'No. Not here.'

They would have to transfer Bo to another ICU, where they could do dialysis, if he did not respond to the second-best treatment they could offer.

Apparently, they do not have a dialysis machine in Loughlinstown. People have dialysis machines in their own homes, supplied to them by the HSE. But this hospital, with its geriatric ward, its A&E, doesn't possess one. It's unconscionable.

Quite predictably, Bo didn't respond to whatever treatment he was offered. At three o'clock the consultant spoke to me on the corridor and told me they were going to transfer him to another hospital. They were in the process of telephoning the various hospitals, asking for a bed in ICU. Vincent's, Tallaght, Beaumont, the Mater.

This is the second-last act of this tragic farce.

They were having no luck getting a bed.

One of the doctors flitted by – she looked tired. I wondered if she had been on duty for eighty hours? Probably.

'That's the trouble at weekends. They keep their beds for accident cases.'

They're hoarding beds? A bed that could save Bo's life?

He's eighty-two.

In Ireland, this matters. You're dispensable.

In Vincent's Private, in the Beacon, in Blackrock, it is not an issue. But in an HSE public hospital, old folk move over to make room for the young. It is a question of resources, I am sure the minister would say. It is a question of resources that they do not have a dialysis machine, which my friend in Kerry has in her own garage, which every local clinic in Sweden has, in this hospital.

Finally a bed was offered in Beaumont.

Far away in Glasnevin. Is it?

I had never been to Beaumont.

But now I was going. The ambulance has been called. Bo is being prepared for the move. I am sitting in the corridor with my coat on, waiting to join him. Two ambulance men go into ICU with a trolley. I think they may be the same ones who brought Bo here on Monday.

I wait.

Minutes pass.

Then the nurse comes out.

'The patient's condition has changed,' she says. 'He cannot be moved now.'

The ambulance men come out.

'Sorry, we don't have the right oxygen equipment in the ambulance,' one of them says. 'If it was just down the N11 to Vincent's we could do it. But over to Beaumont in Friday afternoon traffic? It'd be chaos, in the ambulance.'

They don't have a dialysis machine. The ambulance doesn't have the right equipment. Vincent's is hoarding its beds for the weekend casualties. There's the Friday afternoon traffic.

For the want of a nail the horseshoe was lost.

On their increasingly frequent visits to the green waiting room, doctors talk about transferring Bo later. It's quite obvious that nobody believes this for one second.

In ICU, they change his oxygen supply. Now, instead of a mask which he can take off when it gets too uncomfortable, a plastic tube is inserted through his mouth, down his throat, into his lung. It is held in place with an elastic band that stretches his mouth horribly.

'He is anaesthetised. He feels nothing. No pain,' the nurse assures me.

How do they know?

What I know now is that Bo is going to die.

Bo told me he was not afraid of death.

'But I am afraid of pain,' he said.

'Don't worry,' I said. 'I won't let you feel pain. I won't let anyone hurt you.'

I thought, if Bo's cancer got bad, that we could go to Switzerland, that he would die peacefully. I thought if that did not happen that he would have a comfortable bed in a lovely hospital, that he would have one of those contraptions that allows the patient to inject morphine, that he would die listening to Mozart in the arms of morphia.

But there will be none of that here.

He is trussed up like a turkey for the oven. His eyes are closed, the lids swollen. His mouth is cruelly pulled by the elastic band. I try to loosen it but am afraid I will loosen the tube that penetrates his body like a sword.

A Day of Our Life

Memories are stored as snapshots, flashes in the cortices.

Nine months after we married, we had our first wonderful child, and two years later, our second. We were delighted with our children, and devoted to them, but in retrospect it is clear to me that we missed having a honeymoon period. After the secret relationship, with all its problems, we plunged directly into parenthood with all its challenges. We were good enough parents, and the children turned out well, but life was sometimes stormy. I held down a full-time job that I didn't really want for some of the time, a part-time job for all of it. Bo was full time and then retired. Both of us were committed to writing. There was a constant struggle to find time to fit in everything. For instance, when I went on maternity leave – just three months, in 1983, and officially the first month was supposed to be taken before the child was born – I immediately started writing a novel. When the baby napped, I sat at my typewriter and wrote. Bo too was always anxious to work at his transcriptions, editorial work and articles. This was a desperate need for both of us, and it caused tension and friction. There were ongoing arguments about housework and childcare – I was obsessed by feminism, and aware that it was outrageous that women still did most of the housework. Retrospectively, I know I was right in theory but in practice we would have had a much more pleasant life if I had let those theories go, or if I had relaxed them a little. Quarrelling is such a waste of time.

Could it have been otherwise? Possibly, if I had felt secure enough to give up my job, stay at home, and combine writing and looking after the children. But I didn't feel secure enough. I was always worried about money, even though we always had enough. I was worried about the future. If I gave up my job I might never get another, was my view: Ireland was like that, in the seventies and eighties. There was no flexibility, there was massive unemployment. Apart from all its other downsides, that limits people's freedom. Anyone who has a job stays in it, for fear of never getting another one. Economic paralysis ensues.

I had reason to be careful. Bo, worn down by stress and smoking, had a heart operation just as our first baby was being born – he was in hospital, getting a triple bypass, when I was in hospital giving birth.

From that time I felt afraid that Bo would die.

That he lived for another thirty years was a blessing. But almost every day I was aware that life was precarious – his life. My own I never considered at risk. I was going to live for ever. And actually I had no health problems.

Nor did Bo, after the bypass, until the day in September 2011 when he was diagnosed with prostate cancer.

It's possible to have a career and be a parent, and handle everything efficiently and smoothly. But it is doubtful if it's possible to have two careers and be a parent with ease. That's what I tried to do.

Although I always knew I was in love with Bo, I was not completely happy with our life together until the children were grown up, had left home, and until I had left my job in the National Library and had enough time to write. This happened in 2007, the year my mother died. We had six years of perfect happiness together.

That's lucky.

SATURDAY
DAY 12,000

Thin ice

Marja and I spent Friday night in the green room, sleeping on the slippery sofas, our coats doing duty as quilts. The rest of the family stayed in our house in Shankill. At 6 a.m., the night nurse told us Bo's blood pressure had gone down. Marja phoned Shankill and everyone arrived. We spent Saturday morning in the green room. We took it in turns to go in and out to Bo – I was there most of the time.

At about one, we were all allowed in together.

Bo was stretched on the bed, his eyes closed, his mouth stretched. I had been talking to him all along.

I go on talking. I tell him the story of his own life – all the anecdotes I remember, from his childhood on. He was always telling me about his life so I know the stories very well. About the boys' room and the girls' room and the room where the apples were stored in winter, giving off such an intoxicating fragrance. About his mother who tended a garden full of flowers and fruit – red raspberries and yellow raspberries – who cooked pike and perch with wonderful sauces. About Anderson's Epicerie, the big general store not far from the Almqvists' house in Edsgata. About running wild all summer in the forest with his friend, Yngve. About skiing to school in winter, skating on the lake. Going to school on the train, to Karlstads Läroverk. His first trips away, to Switzerland, Paris, then Iceland and Ireland. I tell him about our holidays together, I describe them, I tell him I love him, I ask him to forgive me for the times I was angry and mean, all those things. We sing 'Santa Lucia'. I sing 'Cuaichín Ghleann Neifín'. I talk and talk. I recite sonnets by Shakespeare. I say Fröding, Fröding, Fröding, now you'll have to supply the rest (this Hanna, Bo's granddaughter, tells me later. Fröding was Bo's favourite poet, partly because he came from the same place as he did, namely the parish of Alster in Värmland. He is, or was, one of the most popular of all Swedish poets, somewhat on a par with Yeats or Kavanagh or Heaney in Ireland.).

At about ten to two the nurse tells us his blood pressure has gone right down.

We kiss him goodbye.

Me, his daughter, his sons, his grandchildren, his in-laws, his nephew Emmet, who has appeared at the last moment.

We are all still there, gathered around the bed, when a doctor comes and tells us that Bo's heart has stopped beating. It stopped at a minute past 2 p.m. on Saturday, 9 November 2013.

I sit with him alone for a while.

Soon I get impatient.

I have lost the battle; what is the point of this? I flounce out of the ICU.

In the dreadful green room, somebody has produced a bottle of whiskey. Although I can understand this, I find it disconcerting. Just minutes ago Bo was alive. But the Irish wake is already beginning.

Ragnar takes my arm and we go back to the car.

I insist on driving.

The petrol tank is close to empty and I also insist on stopping at the garage. Ragnar fills it for me and goes into the cashier while I sit at the wheel, looking at someone driving a Volvo into the big crushing wheels of the carwash. The last time I filled the tank was in Lifford, at Daly's Garage, on the way to Gweedore in the lashing Donegal rain. Bo beside me, reassuring me that we'd probably be in time for dinner with Micheál.

Ragnar comes back and I drive home, in bright November sunshine.

PART TWO

Afterword

The world is full of widows – several among my closer friends.
We have each known that grim rite of passage, have engaged with
grief and loss, and have not exactly emerged, but found a way of
living after and beyond. It is an entirely changed life, for anyone
who has been in a long marriage ... alone in bed, alone most of the
time, without that presence towards which you turned for advice,
reassurance, with whom you shared the good news and the bad.
Every decision now taken alone, no one to diffuse anxieties. And a
thoroughly commonplace experience – everywhere, always, so get on
with it and don't behave as though you are uniquely afflicted.

Penelope Lively, *Ammonites & Leaping Fish. A Life in Time*

Penelope Lively, one of the many writers whose work comforted
me during the first shocking years of grief, describes it succinctly,
but well.

When your spouse or partner, the person who is closest to you
in this world, dies, and especially if they die abruptly, you may go
into a state of shock and denial. As is well known, these reactions
are part of the stages of grief. There is plenty of debate about
the concept of the 'stages' – Elisabeth Kübler-Ross's famous
'five stages' – denial, anger, bargaining, depression, acceptance.
This catalogue originally described the reactions of terminally-
ill patients to their own diagnoses, and was later expanded by
Kübler-Ross to cover responses to many kinds of loss. She herself
questioned her original theory that the affected person moves

chronologically through the various stages, and her concepts in general have been questioned and criticised. Nevertheless they are almost always cited in any work on bereavement and grief. George Bonanno found that the most significant response of the bereaved was 'resilience': they recover to the point where grief is absent. Colin Murray Parkes, in his investigations of bereavement, also notes the role of resilience. A majority of widows investigated by him in a London survey in the 1960s reported improvements in feelings after a year. If considerable improvement was not in place after eighteen months, he suggests that 'complicated grief', rather than 'natural grief', is involved.

The bereaved may experience some or all of the 'stages' of denial, anger, sorrow, acceptance – in a random order. (Bargaining does not seem to fit into the catalogue of emotions for the bereaved; obviously those who are terminally ill or attached to the terminally ill may bargain with God – take me, rather than him, or whatever. But I cannot see a place for bargaining in the catalogue of emotions felt by those whose loved one has died, unless they believe in miracles. If you send him back I will give all my money to the church? It doesn't make sense.) These strong emotions are likely to assault the individual in a series of waves, which overwhelm, then recede. As time moves on, the recessions or gaps become longer, and the waves of strong emotion less intense and easier to cope with. That's the theory, and in my experience, it is more or less accurate.

In the few weeks immediately following Bo's death, I felt the numbness and emotional denial that is described in the literature about bereavement. It seemed to me that I had no feelings at all. Rather, I had a curious sense of being hollow, without anything inside my skin – no stomach, heart, or emotions. Perhaps I was aware, viscerally, that the part of my identity, my personality, myself, which was Bo, had now gone? It was as if my innards had been scooped out and I was like a blown-up plastic doll, empty inside. Or transparent, like a ghost.

On the surface, I assumed I looked and behaved just as usual.

I was surprised at what I was happy to call my 'resilience', the term I quickly picked up from reading Colin Murray Parkes' book. One latches on to any concept that offers hope or comfort.

And certainly one seems resilient, at first. The theory is that the mind shuts down, so the body will have time to adjust to the new situation. This may be an exaggeration of the response, or just a piece of folklore. At first, it seemed that I just didn't have time to absorb the fact of Bo's death - it had come about so suddenly. On Thursday, 7 November, I assumed Bo would recover. On Friday, 8 November, I was still being reassured by medical personnel that he would be okay. On Saturday, 9 November, he was dead. And as is usually the case when someone dies, the first week or two were extremely busy, filled with events and people. My children and their partners stayed in the house; there was a constant stream of visitors, bringing casseroles and cakes and flowers, memories and sympathy. And of course there were visits to the undertakers, decisions to be made about the funeral, a service to be designed. The few weeks around the funeral were as filled with activity and tasks as very busy periods at work – it was not unlike the weeks leading to the opening of a major exhibition in the National Library, or coming up to a conference for which one has had organisational responsibility.

No plans for the funeral were in place since Bo had died unexpectedly. We had on a few occasions talked about death and funerals, but in a light-hearted way. Once, long ago, Bo had asked to be cremated, and to have his ashes scattered in Dunquin Kerry. But in later years he wondered if it would be nice to have a grave, and asked me if I would go and leave flowers on it. 'Are you mad?' I had said. 'I never go to graveyards! I don't like them!' Which was true. Back then. Before.

Now, however, I decided that I would fulfil both requests. Bo could be cremated. Some of his ashes would be buried in the cemetery close to where we live, so he would have a grave and headstone that I could visit and lay flowers on. Later we would scatter the rest of the ashes in his beloved Dunquin.

When Bo died on Saturday, 9 November, the consultant asked if I would agree to a post-mortem examination of the body, an autopsy. I agreed. I would have requested such an examination myself, if it had not been suggested. On Monday, 11 November, somebody telephoned from Loughlinstown and suggested that we skip the post-mortem, on the grounds that it would cause me further upset. But I didn't find the idea upsetting; on the contrary, and I insisted that it go ahead. (Later, the consultant told me he had not authorised the request from the hospital to cancel the autopsy, and he knew nothing about it or why it had been made.) The post-mortem was carried out, and this meant that the funeral was delayed for a week. This did not concern me in the slightest. I needed a week to make all the arrangements, which were complicated since Bo was originally Lutheran, but for most of his life an agnostic, with a strong affection for Irish traditions – including the Irish traditions surrounding funerals. I tried to design a funeral that would honour all his affiliations, and was helped by family and friends to put together a service which was appropriate. In Sweden, Bo's country, it is normal to hold funerals about three weeks after the death, so a week seemed like a reasonable period of waiting to me. I find the Irish tradition, holding the funeral a day or two after the death, almost unseemly in its haste. It is as there is a desire to get the whole thing over with and resume normal life as fast as possible. Since for the widow, normal life will not be resuming any time soon, if ever, there is really no rush.

I don't think I cried at all during that week, or at the funeral. A non-stop party was going on in my house. I was constantly aware that the most important person, for me, was missing, but the atmosphere was lively. Somebody gave me Xanax and I slept reasonably well. I could eat. There was little time to ponder what had happened. Even when I did, I could not believe that Bo was really dead. The phrase 'I don't believe it!', uttered so often, in Ireland, in response to any surprising news, made perfect sense. I didn't believe it. My body insisted that Bo was just away somewhere, on a trip abroad, or in Kerry, and would come back soon if I just hung on. He had to come back. How could it be otherwise? The arrangements – Which sort of coffin? Cremation or burial? Where will we have the service? – seemed to relate to someone else, some stranger. The funeral seemed like a toy funeral, a weird game that for some reason I was obliged to play. It was held in the small church in Belfield, since Belfield had been such a key locus in our lives, and everyone said it was a lovely service. Even during it, I felt no emotion, apart from a mild impatience with the whole thing and a wish to be elsewhere – at home with Bo. After the cremation in Mount Jerome, as people came and offered their condolences, I found myself looking over my shoulder, wondering where he was. I had had enough, as he or I often had at a party. It was time to escape, get into the car, go home and have a chat about the social event we'd just been at, and then return to our normal lives.

One of the things I miss most is the possibility of relaxing totally with Bo, chatting frankly and ironically about the party or the lecture or the visit or the funeral. And then going back to reading and writing companionably, cooking and eating, watching the nine o'clock news.

After about two weeks the fuss died down. My children went back to their own places and occupations. I was alone in the house. Good friends, especially two of Bo's good friends, Pádraig and Roibeard, telephoned me every few days, to make sure I was all right, and my sister and some of my own friends were in frequent contact. But my sense of transparency and hollowness increased. I felt as if I were made of paper, moving through the rooms like a shadow, and the house seemed large and cold and alien. What was I doing here? I had hardly ever been in the house without Bo for longer than a few weeks.

After two or three weeks, the soft grief, the tears, began to hit. The metaphors – waves, inundation, floods – are accurate. Grief dissolves you. I could no longer sleep upstairs in our bed; the big bedroom overlooking the sea was cold and frightening. I took to sleeping on the sofa in the front room. In the mornings I woke with a tight knot in my stomach, and rocked myself in bed for half an hour before I could get up. In my diary I described the sensations of grief, ad nauseam – they lasted for several months:

> This is how grief feels: there is a heaviness in the chest. An iron ring around the heart. Tears on the bubble behind the eyes. Sometimes an empty feeling in the stomach.

> All these feelings can go away temporarily. But they return, as if the ring around the heart were the default position for the body.

I began to panic about financial issues. There were many forms to fill in, at a time when the last thing I wanted to do was this sort of work. There was actually no immediate financial problem. But even when everything was sorted out the household income had been more than halved overnight, although all the main expenses remained the same. I didn't know how or if I would manage. As it happens, everything fell into place gradually and this is no longer a problem, but dealing with a new economy and a new – lower – income is one of the issues, one of the immediate losses, that widows face and that adds to the terror of the experience, and this aspect of the new life is seldom discussed. Bo always helped me deal with worries of this and of any kind, reassuring me that everything would work out, and helping in practical ways: he was efficient at paying bills and so on although he was an unworldly person. Now, when I was down, I was faced with many bureaucratic issues and had nobody to help me deal with them.

I began to have difficulties sleeping. All night I would relive the last week of Bo's life – the pills, the rash, the argument about the private hospital. I could not get the image of Bo trussed up like a turkey, intubated, his mouth pulled to one side cruelly, out of my head. I was convinced he had suffered pain. I went over all the mistakes I had made. If I had done A or B or C, Bo would be alive. If I had insisted on doing what I knew was right, if I had shouted louder and got him out of the hospital. I had promised Bo that I would make sure he never suffered pain. But he had suffered great pain, in the end. I had stood by and let this happen.

I went to a doctor and got some sleeping pills. I began to visit a counsellor, who listened sympathetically to my story and did not dismiss my version of events in the hospital as just a 'stage of grief' – denial, or anger. I continued to visit her for six months and the sessions became a crucial part of my survival during that time.

I developed a strategy, although develop is hardly the *mot propre*, to 'get through'. Grief is a rusting of the soul, which only work and the passage of time will scour away, Dr Johnson said, or words to that effect. He also said that grief will pass, but the suspense – the waiting – is terrible. I delved into all the grief literature I could find. Some of it helped. Most of it offered some word of useful advice. One writer gave hope, another wisdom, yet another simply the comfort of empathy: understanding that other people went through this too – half the world, in fact – for some reason provided consolation, although I don't really know why. Misery likes bedfellows? Or perhaps knowing that they experienced this trauma but survived to write about it suggested that it was possible to 'get through it' and come out the other side, if not 'healed', at least less of a total wreck than one feels in the first months. C.S. Lewis writes that you emerge like a person who has lost a leg. The wound heals and you learn to manage without it. In my raw state, to paraphrase Julian Barnes, I felt as if I had been thrown out of an aeroplane so that seemed realistic, even optimistic. I think it was simply the company of the bereaved that one experiences in these good books which was in itself a comfort – the knowledge, in their accounts of the last days of their loved ones and the days, early and late, of their grieving, that somebody understood what losing your spouse is like. They 'get it': these writers who have done us the service of describing their own loss and sorrow. As did my many neighbours and friends who had been widowed themselves, who 'belonged to the club nobody wants to be a member of', as Dermot Bolger, a writer who lost his wife a few years back, put it in his letter of condolence. The main comfort of those books was in their richness of insight and understanding: Joyce Carol Oates's *A Widow's Story*, Julian Barnes's *Levels of Life*, C.S. Lewis's *A Grief Observed*, Joan Didion's *The Year of Magical Thinking*. Henning Mankell's collection of essays, *Kvicksand* – several of which deal not with bereavement but with his reaction to his cancer diagnosis – I found particularly uplifting. There is plenty of rubbish among the self-help books, many of which I bought – you see quickly which work is good and which superficial. I found research-based studies of grief by psychologists and psychiatrists useful. In particular, Colin Murray Parkes's study of grief in widows was comforting – *Bereavement: Studies of Grief in Adult Life* (1972). This is a scientific study of the process of grief, but it's written in accessible prose. Conclusions, such as that after eighteen months 70 per cent of widows reported significant improvement in their feelings, offered more hope than statements such as 'everyone's grief is different', or 'it comes in waves' – true as these observations are. Eighteen months seemed like a long time to suffer the sorrow and sense of loss I was experiencing, as I realised more and more that Bo and I were soulmates, and that there is nobody in the world who shares my particular interests and perspective on life as he did. But at least the statistics suggested that recovery was possible, that people are resilient.

Ordinary proverbial wisdom, folk wisdom, also suggested that recovery was likely, of course. On a dark day in January, soon after the beginning of the spring term, I bumped into Bo's old friend and colleague Séamas Ó Catháin on the campus in Belfield. He was about to give a lecture to the Folklore of Ireland Society. I burst into tears, as I was doing repeatedly at this time whenever anyone said a sympathetic word or even gave me a kind look.

'I know it's a cliché,' Séamas said, 'but time will make it easier.'

'It's a cliché, but it is a true cliché,' my friend Luz Mar Gonzales Arias wrote, in one of her many comforting emails. 'Time heals.'

And a neighbour I met while walking in Shankill put some sort of time limit on it. She, who had been widowed when she was a young mother of three children, said, 'It takes a few years to get over it.' This was when I had been widowed for a few weeks. A few years sounded like a death sentence. But I held on to her words. I could believe her, because she was in the club nobody wants to belong to. She had gone through it and survived.

I was advised by others, including my counsellor, not to set time limits. In fact, the counsellor in particular had an aversion to time limits, and hinted that I was too obsessed with that idea. But clinging to the belief that it will get better in time is a comfort. We need hope and the only hope for someone who is shattered by the death of their partner is that there is light at the end of the tunnel, that time will heal. One hears different time limits.

'Four years' – said my friend Helena, who had watched her mother recover from the untimely death of her father – 'after four years you could sense a lightening, a change'.

Of course it is true that the waves of grief return, even over two years later, and a pang of longing can ambush you when you least expect it. But the most terrible waves do not return as often as in the first year, and when they do they are easier to deal with.

For instance, after about a year I stopped reliving the last horrific days of Bo's life; perhaps until then I had been going over every moment of that nightmare of a week, in some vain expectation of correcting the mistakes, doing things differently, and arriving at a different result: life rather than death. It was what Joan Didion calls 'magical thinking'; you relive the past in order to change it. But you can't change the past. We know that but the subconscious, the body, doesn't get the message. It took about a year for the lesson to sink in. It was a year before I stopped obsessively going over the most horrible week of my life. After two or three years, I stopped thinking about Bo all the time. After three years, I was able to think about him without sadness – I can simply remember him; I consult him for advice, and, although this can obviously be self-deceptive, I feel fairly confident in almost all instances of what his advice to me would be. I had in any case been in the habit of talking to my mother, who died in 2007, in this way: as far as both she and Bo are concerned, I can guess what their counsel would be, and in both instances I know they are always on my side.

Of course, talking to a memory or a ghost is not the same as talking to a living person. A good imagination is a gift, but it can be overrated. As Keats wrote, imagination is no substitute for the real thing. 'The fancy cannot cheat so well/ As she is fam'd to do, deceiving elf.' You get used to it, walking with one leg. There is no compensation for the loss. With Bo, I shared a great deal: a love of nature, walking, holidays, exploring, books, various modern and medieval languages, folklore, history, literature, our garden, our house, our children. Certain television programmes. There is nobody in the world with the same eclectic combination of talents and feelings and interests. I know nobody who is as truly learned and who wears his learning so lightly (although my sons are contenders, possibly). I feel his absence constantly. But it hurts less, even as I gain ever more insight into how much we had together and how unique and special and perhaps strange our marriage was.

It took a few years before I could walk down a street in Dingle, where we used to go on holidays, without weeping. During my first visits to Kerry, in 2014, this was not possible. I missed him every second of the day in Dunquin and the surroundings. I would park my car in the car park near the mart in Dingle, and walk down to Main Street and Green Street, and break down in tears. Always we had parked, then gone our separate ways for an hour or so – while I shopped and went to the Internet Cafe to check my emails. We would meet in Cafe Liteartha, where Bo would be engaged in conversation with someone, or just reading and drinking coffee, and then we'd drive home. These were very simple pleasures, but afternoons of real happiness – my only consolation was that I was aware of how happy I was while experiencing those times. But it took a long time before walking around Dingle alone brought me anything other than pain.

One is advised to 'live through the grief', not to avoid it or try to bat it away. There is not a lot of choice – grief waylaid me in predictable and unpredictable ways. I hate words like 'wallowing' or 'self-pity'. They are judgemental and used by those who have a tendency to dismiss and deny emotional pain – yes, it would be great if it did not exist, but unfortunately it does. And of course you wallow in sorrow when you lose your husband. Of course you feel self-pity, as well as pity for him. How could it be otherwise? I do not have a stiff upper lip, nor do I want one. I 'went through it'. But I needed also to find ways of escaping from it. If you 'went through it' from morning to night and morning again, your life would not be worth living. You would drown in sorrow. And some do.

I quickly began to look for ways of temporary escape. I noticed already in the first month that while I was teaching a class, on the short story or the novel, I felt no sadness: all my attention was focussed on the students and the texts we were discussing. After my class, in Belfield, going back up the stairs, I would feel horribly empty, and suffer huge pangs of sorrow. Woe betide anyone who bumped into me on the stairs – they would be treated to a spate of tears. Everyone was of course entirely kind and sympathetic, but it must have been embarrassing or frightening for them sometimes. Usually they asked, kindly, 'Would you like a cup of tea?'

Belfield was strongly linked to Bo in my heart. I had met him there, and all through our life we had been in and out of the college. It was part of our ordinary personal landscape. Very often after my class we met outside the Folklore Department, and we then had lunch together in the canteen. If I was late Bo would telephone. Now I went up the grey stairs alone. Bo would not phone to ask, what's keeping you?

Soon after Bo's death, one of the things several people said was 'Be kind to yourself'. Lots of empty formulae and annoying comments are iterated to new widows ('Call me if there's anything I can do', 'We must have lunch sometime', 'What age was he?') but this is one of the most irritating, and puzzling. Whenever I heard it, my immediate thought was 'Wouldn't it be better if you were kind to me?' But I wasn't even sure what the phrase was supposed to mean, and I don't think those who trot it out knew either. When I asked someone for clarification, she was clearly taken aback, then shrugged and said, 'Well, have a massage. Eat a whole box of chocolates if you feel like it.' Ah, yes! Possibly the advice about the massage – very common – was not bad, in that it acknowledges that the body suffers grief as well as the mind. Grief is visceral; the emotions and the physique are affected alike. Hence the knot in the stomach, the tightness in the chest.

After a while I interpreted 'Be kind to yourself' as finding out what I really liked to do and allowing myself to do it.

I set myself goals and tasks in fields that I liked. Easy tasks for the most part, but tasks that I knew would require concentration. I enrolled for an online course in Swedish writing, since my writing skills in the language were poor: I learnt to write Danish correctly in 1978 but although I had made the transition to oral Swedish decades ago and even though I read Swedish regularly my spelling and grammar when I wrote were not good – surprisingly, I seem to be able to read endlessly and still not write the language accurately, possibly because I tend to read fast. I continued to write book reviews regularly for the *Irish Times* – they continued to ask for them, which was a real blessing. I wrote a diary and kept a record of dreams. In the summer, I took a summer course on Irish grammar in Kerry – I realised that doing a course would help me to come to terms with being in Dunquin without Bo, which was a huge challenge, since, in thirty years, I had never been in our house down there without him, and since, over the past six or seven years, our summers there had been idyllic. In 2015 I began to learn a new language, Bulgarian. It's very hard to sink into grief when dealing with the aspect of the verb in a Slavonic language, or trying to pronounce a new word of ten syllables.

I also watched a lot of films. I found out how to get Swedish TV programmes on the internet and watch them on my TV set, and I saw many drama series that interested me; this was an easy way to keep in touch with the Swedish language, which went out of my everyday life with Bo. I went for long walks alone and with a group, swam once or twice a week. I socialised with my good friends, and made some new friends – wonderful people, actively kind – during this time.

For the first year, though, my only goal was to survive. After that I would start working properly again. Joyce Carol Oates in her moving account of her own first year of widowhood confirmed that. 'On the first anniversary of her husband's death, the widow should congratulate herself. I have survived.' That is enough, for the first year.

My interest in writing fiction vanished completely, although I continued to read it, and some novels were directly comforting (especially those by the Brontës, who were so acquainted with death and grief). But the creation of fiction seemed trivial, like a pointless child's game. When, after a year, I took on commissions to write I tended to write autobiographically, about death, since everything else seemed irrelevant and insignificant.

The counsellor was adamant that I had to allow grief to take its time and its toll. At her sessions, I wept copiously, to the extent that I worried about her capacity to stand all my crying. But she was unfailingly sympathetic and encouraging.

'You can't believe this now,' she said. 'But one day you will look in the mirror and feel a lightening of spirit.'

As with the cliché about time's healing processes, I stored

this, or it stored itself, in my memory. I don't think I have felt that lightening even yet. But I have had many enjoyable experiences, and wonderful relationships – especially with my new grandchildren, Freja, Niko and Sadhbh. 'Present pleasures are no replacement for past joys,' Julian Barnes writes in *Levels of Life*. Joy is difficult to feel, in the absence of the love of one's life. But it is in any case always elusive and becomes rarer as we get older. Like grief, or death, joy visits us, but it is impossible to make a reservation for a minute or hour or day of joy. It obeys no commands. A more everyday contentment is something we can strive for, however, and manage to achieve.

My life is fairly privileged. I am not well off but I have enough money to live on, my adult children still live in Dublin and are warm and supportive. I have many good friends. Teaching creative writing has always been engaging and enjoyable, and during the first year of Bo's absence was a reliable harbour in the stormy ocean of grief. I have written this memoir at home on my sofa in Shankill, but also at various residences in other centres for artists and writers – Haihatus, in Joutsa in Finland; the Baltic Centre for Writers and Translators in Visby, in Sweden; and the Tyrone Guthrie Centre in Annaghmakerrig.

'Be kind to yourself.'

It all helps.

Dreams

Unlike Orpheus, we can no longer descend to the Underworld in search of our lost spouses, nor can I hope to ascend to an Overworld where Bo waits for me with open arms. Dead is dead, I believe. As Julian Barnes points out in his account of bereavement, we can descend into our memories and into our dreams. Dreams are particularly analogous to another numinous world, since we have no control over them. You can buy a ticket to China or New Zealand, but when you fall asleep you go on a mystery tour, and who knows who you will meet in the place where you may find yourself. A place that is almost always both vaguely familiar and somewhat strange, a mixture of the known and unknown.

In the first weeks I was surprised and disappointed that my dreams about Bo were few, or nonexistent. For six weeks, he did not come to me in my dreams, at all, although I thought about him during all my waking moments.

The first time he came was around Christmas, when I was staying with Ragnar and Ailbhe, for a night, in their house in Stoneybatter. In the dream Bo hugged me tightly, and said, 'I wish we could be together for a hundred years.'

Dreams express desires, as Nadezhda, my other daughter-in-law and a psychoanalyst, points out.

After that, Bo began to come to me in dreams quite frequently. Some of the dreams were filled with love, but many were at least tinged with anxiousness about his survival. For instance, this dream, which I had on 20 January:

We were walking in a park, covered in snow. Bo was nevertheless dressed in his usual tweed jacket, checked shirt and tweed tie – no coat. It wasn't cold. There was no temperature, actually – I don't feel hot or cold in dreams, just neutral. We were happy but in the normal way, happy walking together. Ahead of us was a hill or cliff of snow. I began to throw snowballs, trying to get them to go over the edge of this cliff. Bo laughed at me. Mostly I could not get the snowballs to go over the edge.

Then I was at the other side of the ledge – more like a snowy plateau, snowier and more open than where we'd been before. Bo was throwing snowballs now. He came over the edge of the hill. I said, don't do that. I could see that the snow was fragile, like thin ice. I felt he was in danger. And sure enough the snow gave way, and he sank into it and was covered in snow. I managed to get him out. His eyes were closed but he was breathing and I knew he was alive. Perfectly dressed, looking quite normal, lying in the snow.

There were other people in the background but they didn't come to us.

The part of the dream where we walked was comforting. It was comforting to dream of Bo at all. But now that I write it down I see I am rehearsing the panic, the danger, the fall. Bo fell and I thought I could rescue him on my own, but I couldn't.

Later, in March, I had a dream in which I suddenly remembered that Bo was dead:

I was in my own bed, our bed. Where I actually was. Something was nibbling my toe. I thought, a mouse. Bo said something comforting, some jokey thing, or I had a sense of Bo saying the sort of comforting, ironic thing he would have, in such a situation. I had a sense of being in bed on a Sunday morning, in a joking relaxed mood, as we must have been on hundreds and hundreds of occasions during our life.

But as I felt the Sunday morning feeling I remembered that Bo was dead. I grabbed his jumper – which is in fact in the bed still – and cried bitterly.

Subsequently, over the past two years, I have had dreams in which the opposite occurs: I discover that Bo is still alive, and that he never died. In January 2016, I had a dream of this kind:

In a town, in a house, with my sister, Síle, and some others. I go out – down winding stairs, as in a tower. Walk through the town, not a place I know. We pass a row of houses with green gardens in front. In each garden a man is cutting the grass. In one of the gardens, which is slightly different from the others because a space to park a car has been made in it, at the front, Bo is cutting the grass. We pass him and Síle says he looks tired. We discuss this and I remember that he never felt tired when he came to Kerry in the past (this is apparently in Kerry, although it has been defamiliarised, it doesn't look at all like Dunquin, or even like Dingle). He always arrived after the long journey full of energy. We think the difference is that his friends are not here any more, all dead, and that's why he's tired. I go back to the garden. Bo is lying on the grass, having a rest. I joke with him that he's lazy. We laugh. He looks very tall, very handsome, very much as he was when we were first together, and for most of the time. I am impressed by how handsome he looks. He's wearing his beige summer trousers and a white shirt. He's about fifty or sixty in this image. I think, but Bo, everyone thinks you are dead. We have had a funeral, with a coffin. There have been tributes and obituaries. Yet here you are alive, stretched out on the grass. I feel anxious about how we can reconcile these two narratives, that Bo is dead and that Bo is actually alive. I am a bit confused, but happy to be with him. We must have made a mistake, thinking he was dead.

And again, on 22 July 2017:

We – my children and I – are going to an event, a concert or performance of some kind. New shoes are needed. I try on the shoes in a shoe shop, telling the assistant that we only have twenty-three minutes to get them. The shoes are lovely – brown with cream spots. When I go to pay, the owner of the shop asks if I am the person who made the tapestry in the shop. Yes. Then you do not have to pay, he tells me.

We sit at the front of the hall or perhaps church where the event is to take place. All in a row. Bo arrives. He looks himself, aged about fifty or sixty. Cheerful, nicely dressed. He comes to our pew and hugs me for a long time. We are all delighted that he has come back, that he is not dead, or that he has resurrected.

The next day there is an article in the newspaper, written by a journalist who had apparently been sitting just behind us. 'Family surprised when husband returns from the dead' is the headline.

'Our father goes early to bed, for he is an old man'

Anger is one of the Kübler-Ross stages. You can feel anger towards yourself, towards the dead person, or towards other people. I never felt angry at Bo. It was not his fault that he died. He was the victim of the fumbling of others, which is tragic, for Bo was above all painstaking and conscientious, in all his work and all that he did. He did not take shortcuts and had a deep sense of responsibility and duty. I felt angry towards myself, for my various bad decisions: not to read the instructions on the packet of pills; not to get him to a good hospital while there was still time; not to know about facilities such as private ambulances; and finally to agree to send him to Loughlinstown.

Anger at medical personnel is not uncommon, among the bereaved. I was furious with several doctors. I've read studies of grief, so I considered the possibility that this reaction was largely emotional, hysterical. But I am a rational person, and a person who has been trained – by Bo – to think clearly and to rely on evidence. I observed at first hand the way Bo was treated in the hospital, and kept notes even while I was there sitting at his bedside. Failures of care and attention occurred from the beginning, from the moment when the ambulance men had him walk down the drive – I saw the shock and surprise in the ambulance men's faces when Bo almost collapsed from the effort and pain after the short walk. The confusion as to whether he was in the hospital or not when I arrived there on Monday evening did not inspire confidence in the standards of record-keeping. That the A&E staff did not begin the process of hydration as soon as he was admitted, but left him lying for hours without even a glass of water, was dismaying. The sloppiness about the intravenous drip; the unhelpfulness of individuals and the system in facilitating his transfer to another hospital early in that fateful week; and the horrendous last day when they could not get a bed for him in a hospital with dialysis facilities convinced me that my anger was not irrational. I suspected more and more that a lack of adequate care had been a factor leading to Bo's death.

Minor administrative errors that I remembered or that came to my attention in the weeks following Bo's death bolstered my suspicion that there was a general lack of attention to detail in the way the hospital was run. For instance, the unexpected request to cancel the post-mortem examination on Monday 11 November seemed strange, given that the consultant who had recommended the post-mortem had not been aware of this phone call. Who suggested it? Why? The right hand did not seem to know what the left hand was doing. And of course that request begged the question, was there something the hospital wished to hide?

Another cause for uneasiness occurred three weeks after the funeral. I received a bill for Bo's nights in hospital – in Ireland public patients pay 75 euro per night for a hospital stay in a public hospital if they don't have a medical. However, patients who are covered by private health insurance don't pay – the bill is sent directly to the insurance company. Bo had full private insurance. When I telephoned the accounts department querying the bill the official said, 'Oh, he is registered as a public patient. We didn't know he was private.' I recalled then that on the night of Monday, 4 November, when I was at the admissions counter outside A&E, I had said to the official at the desk that Bo had VHI cover (private health insurance). I was told, 'Oh, that doesn't matter here.' If he had been correctly registered would a greater range of hospitals have been available to him, on the last day? Blackrock Clinic, for instance, was much closer than Beaumont. 'Over to Beaumont in Friday afternoon traffic? It'd be chaos,' the ambulance man had said to me. But they could not have contacted Blackrock since they believed Bo was not covered for it by insurance. He was incorrectly registered at the point of admission.

I detailed my questions in a long letter to the consultant, which I copied to our GP. The GP responded a month later, sympathetically. The consultant responded promptly and arranged a meeting to deal with my concerns. He was friendly and helpful.

'I hate the words "What if?" he said. 'If things had turned out differently, you would not be asking these questions.'

Well, obviously not. He explained Bo's deterioration as a 'cascade'. Once it started, with the ingestion of the three pills, it could not be stopped.

My solicitor, who recognised my distress and listened to my doubts, took advice from a barrister who specialises in medical negligence cases. The latter recommended that I commission a report from an expert. I did so – slowly, I must admit. Something held me back, and I did not want to incur large expenses. But on the other hand I wanted to get answers.

In October 2015 the detailed report arrived. I will not reproduce it here. The medical expert found that 'there was failure to treat Professor Almqvist'. He was critical of the delay in giving fluid resuscitation. 'A standard procedure would be to give intravenous fluids within one hour to restore his circulating fluid volume, restore his blood pressure, and hopefully restore a good urine output allowing correction of renal failure. His initial litre of fluid was not started until three hours after admission.'

The report found that Bo had suffered from sepsis, which was not identified until after his death. 'I do not think the source of sepsis could have been identified at the point of admission, but should have been considered as soon as blood results were available. At that point a vigorous search for a source of sepsis should have been initiated and he should have been started on a suitable potent broad spectrum antibiotic pending results of investigations.'

Bo's organ failure came about as a result of sepsis, which was neither identified nor treated in the hospital.

The broad conclusion was that 'if optimally managed he on balance of probability would have survived at worst a 20–25% 30-day mortality and a 75%–80% chance of surviving'.

Bo was not 'optimally managed'. Any fool could see that, and the expert opinion confirmed my impressions. Simple solutions – timely delivery of intravenous fluids, timely administering of an antibiotic – would in all probability have saved his life.

My solicitor said he had never seen such a clear-cut case. 'It's black and white. He had an 80 per cent chance of survival.' He advised suing the hospital. In the event, I decided not to pursue the case. Although I knew my solicitor would only give good advice, I did not want the issue to drag on, and, more than that, I feared the consequences of losing the case. I had no idea how much the case would cost if I lost and had to pay my own legal costs as well as those of the HSE. The solicitor was certain I would win, and pointed out that it would be in the public interest to proceed with the case. But the health service continues to deteriorate, so I am not sure how useful that particular exercise really is.

The HSE could not give me what I want: my husband. Do I blame the hospital for his death? Bo was eighty-two – there seems to be a consensus in Ireland that once you pass eighty you belong to the category 'old', the subtext of which can be 'dispensable'. ('He is old,' as one of the doctors I met in Loughlinstown said so ominously.) 'Old' is a moveable feast, however, and in Sweden eighty is certainly not considered 'dispensable'. Of course he was going to die sometime, as we all are. Nothing is truer than the proverb which warns that nobody knows where the sod of his death is. But Bo had recovered from serious illnesses, he was cancer-free, he had a strong constitution, and hoped to live for several more years – he was working on two major books, which he wanted to finish, and he enjoyed life. He had renewed his passport – but he never got to use it. Bo did not have to die on 9 November 2013. He died as if he had been run over by a bus – and the bus was the Irish health system. Had he been in his own country, or in a competent hospital in Ireland, it is more than likely that he would have survived the episode that killed him – 70–80 per cent likely, according to the impartial medical report. As it was, Bo suffered an untimely, painful, and unnecessary death. It is difficult for me not to think of the Irish public health service – sloppy, careless, and ageist – as a murder machine.

In one of his essays Henning Mankell writes about the *vak*, a patch of thin ice on a frozen lake. If you step on to a *vak* while skating or walking on the ice, you will sink under the ice and drown in the freezing water. It is almost impossible to rescue a person who is unlucky enough to step on a *vak*.

Bo stepped on the weak spot in the health service. The thin ice gave way. He was pulled to the bottom, and I could not rescue him.

Hidden Pictures from the Middle Ages

My relationship with Bo had begun in the Middle Ages, in our shared love of literature, written and oral, old and new. It was a journey in time, and also in place. Our first holiday together was in Denmark, in Copenhagen and on Jutland, where we followed the footsteps of the great nineteenth-century folklore collector, Evald Tang Kristensen. Coincidentally, although we did not know it was the final trip, our last holiday abroad was also in Denmark – on the island of Bornholm and then for a few days in Copenhagen. In that sense, admittedly rather a trivial sense, a circle closed neatly.

I decided, in the year after Bo's death, to visit Scandinavia. It would, of course, have been difficult to go to all the places I had been to with Bo, but in 2014 and 2015 I went to Iceland, Sweden, Norway, Denmark and Finland. In most of these places I was hosted by good friends who understood that I would want to maintain my contacts with the Nordic world. My friend Ulla in Uppsala raised my heart when she said, 'You are always welcome to Sweden.' My other good friends, Helena Wulff and Ulf Hannerz, Marianne Isaaksson in Stockholm, Marian Connolly Andersen in Frederikssund in Denmark, Sirri and Eggert Asgeirsson in Reykjavik, welcomed me to their homes and countries. My fear that without Bo I would lose Scandinavia, its culture and language, was assuaged.

One of the places I visited was Visby on the island of Gotland in the Baltic. I had never been there with Bo, and I went mainly because there is a writers' centre in Visby – the Baltic Centre for Writers and Translators. Much of this memoir was written in the centre. I had not realised how delightful Gotland was, before my visit. I thought it the most beautiful place in the world. When I returned from the island, my sister, Síle, who had visited Visby with her husband when on a Baltic cruise a few years earlier, told me that after she'd been there Bo had said exactly the same thing. 'It is the most beautiful place in the world.' This confirmation that we had independently shared exactly the same opinion was very gratifying. Of course, it must be a common viewpoint.

I was happy in Visby, in the summer of 2015. As well as writing, I went for long walks along the seafront, I cycled to Högklint, where the beach is rich with fossils, with Helena Wulff, who came over from Stockholm to join me for a few days.

One of my happiest days in 2015, a year and a half after Bo's death, was the day I cycled to Hejdeby to find Hejdeby Church.

I leave the medieval walled city of Visby by the eastern gate, cycle across the footbridge over the moat, and then through ordinary garden suburbs until I reach one of the roundabouts. The road to take is the 147, which leads eventually to somewhere called Slite.

There's a cycle path for about two kilometres outside town. I smell the sweet perfume that often tinctures the air around Visby – a light floral bouquet is how it would be described on a perfume bottle. Chicory, cornflowers, chrysanthemums, poppies and meadowsweet flourish on the roadside, but I'm not sure where the smell comes from – from none of those perhaps? From all of them? From some shrub? Some mimosa or jasmine?

It's delicious, this scent, and both more delicate and more definite than any manufactured perfume. Words like evanescent, airy, heady, come to mind. Ephemeral, fleeting, evasive. Numinous: it comes and goes like a fairy or a ghost.

After a few kilometres the real cycle lane stops. For another three or four kilometres there's a hard shoulder, a narrow hard shoulder, and I cycle on this. The landscape becomes scrubby. I'm cycling through a forest of low pine trees. Cars speed along the two-lane road. From the perspective of someone on a bike, they seem to drive very fast. Most of the drivers are polite and give you a wide berth. Occasionally someone, seeing an oncoming car, and unaware that a driver is allowed to slow down, even stop and wait, skims too close for comfort. There's not a lot of traffic but it's fairly constant. Every minute or two a car passes.

Then the hard shoulder stops and I have to cycle on the road, share it with the cars. Just like in Ireland, where I don't cycle. My hands grip the handlebars very tightly, as if this could protect me.

There's nothing along this road for six or seven kilometres. Just the road, the cars, the trees and a sort of scrubland. Not a house or a farm to be seen. Or the cafe I'd been hoping for, somewhere 'on the way'.

Hejdeby. Of course. '*Röslein auf der Heiden.*' This is a heath. The name should warn you.

I wish I'd eaten lunch. I wish I'd brought something to eat in my bag. Luckily I had the sense to put in a bottle of water. And one square of chocolate. I don't feel hungry but it's almost three o'clock and I had breakfast at eight.

Am I on the right road?

The landscape changes. The woodland gives way to fields of corn, of wheat or rye. I see the roof of a house. And then, rising from cushions of fluffy trees, the slim black spire of a church.

Minutes later the sign 'Hejdeby' appears.

The church, just down a little road to the right, is perfect. The snow-white walls, the black roof, the square tower with the black spire on top, the little vestry or altar place tacked on at the back like a kitchen extension. It's set in a green lawn. The graveyard nestling around it, graves dotted like children on the grass. Behind, a field of golden corn.

One car in a parking spot. I cycle along a grass path and park the bike under an elm tree. There are black doors in the white wall and I fear the church may be closed. But it's not.

It was worth the ten kilometre cycle.

Inside, the walls of the church are covered with pale pastel chalk paintings. The twelve apostles. The Virgin Mary. King Solomon riding to Jerusalem. Pale faded pinks, blues, yellows, drawn in two dimensions on the chalk walls.

The pews have painted red roses, framed in blue, on the little gates: you open the gate to gain access to your seat. The pulpit is similarly decorated, and painted blue and red and gold.

Hejdeby Church was built in 1281. After the Reformation, its murals were painted over: the word, not graven images, would hold sway from henceforth in the Lutheran church.

The church was built on sand. This was discovered or attended to in the early twentieth century, and various attempts were made to secure its foundations. In 1995 the floor was taken up. Underneath in the foundations a hoard of silver coins was found – coins that had been placed there, for good luck, when the church was built. More spectacularly, the thick chalky whitewash on the walls was removed, to reveal the most sensational set of murals in any church on Gotland. But many generations of Hejdeby people knew the paintings were there, hidden under the white chalk. They had caught a glimpse of them, through the veil of whitewash, when the sun was strong enough to X-ray the paint, to render it diaphanous. But in the late 1990s they were uncovered, after five hundred years in hiding, sleeping like the princess in the fairy tale.

The church is very simple. The paintings are light, not heavy-handed as later ecclesiastical paintings in other parts of the world can be. Folk art. The design of the church – like all the Gotland churches – is symmetrical, pleasing. The paintings are rather childish, like the art we call naive.

I feel a sense of mystery in this church. It's a small achievement, to have figured out how to get to it, to have reached it on a bicycle. I don't quite feel a direct link to the generations that have sat here, to the people who built and painted the church in the thirteenth century – even before Chaucer was born, for instance. When I was young, I felt, or imagined, such nebulous connections. I felt them in Gortahork in 1978, when I listened to Joe Mac Eachmharcaigh telling his stories.

> There was no word for this: for the sense of being awestruck, of hearing the voices, many voices, of the past, transmuted over centuries. It was like listening to the dead, although the story was as alive as the dogs barking in the winter townlands, or the waves crashing against Bloody Foreland. It was like meeting the poets of the thirteenth century, and every century since then. It was like touching an invisible glinting chain that goes back through the ages, and getting an electric shock from it: small, thrilling, like the shock from some sea creature in the depths of the ocean.

Now I try to regain feelings of that kind, feelings that came easily and spontaneously when I was in my twenties, starting my journey. But they elude me. Sensitivity diminishes with age. Nevertheless I feel something for which I have no adequate words, as I sit on the old painted pew in the dim, silent, clean church. Appreciation. Gratitude. Delight that such a building, such a church, exists, sitting out here in the middle of the summer fields, preserved intact since 1281, in spite of the battles, the Reformation, the tribulations, the economic upheavals, of the centuries.

It's awesome that our world contains such places. Of about a hundred medieval churches on Gotland, more than eighty survive and still function.

There was a sign saying 'Prylbutik 300 metres'. I cycle around but can't find anything. It would be nice to sit here, in the sunshine, on the bench that has been thoughtfully placed close to the church, overlooking the cornfield, and eat a sandwich. (Later I realise that 'Prylbutik' means a sort of flea market, a junk shop; it probably opens only at weekends, when people like to root around and find old things.) Hejdeby seems to be nothing but a townland, containing the church, a farm or two, a house.

So I cycle back to Visby, the walled medieval city, where there are supermarkets and restaurants and nice places to eat.

Acknowledgements

Some of this memoir was written at the Tyrone Guthrie Centre, Annaghmakerrig; The Baltic Centre for Writers and Translators, Gotland; and the Haihatus Artists' Residence, Joutsa, Finland.

Thanks to Helena Wulff, who read the manuscript and made suggestions, and to my editor, Patsy Horton of Blackstaff Press.